WHEN THE FIRE FALLS

BY REX & LOIS BURGHER

WHEN THE FIRE FALLS

Copyright © 2015 by Rex & Lois Burgher

ISBN number: 978-1-935765-14-1

Requests for information should be addressed to:

Lois & Rex Burgher
Kingdom Life Ministry
P O Box 583
Dillsburg, PA
USA 17019

Phone: 717-502-0343
E-mail: info@klifemin.org
Web site: http://www.klifemin.org

Cover Picture, Saint Mary's Lake, Glacier Park, Montana

1st Edition

All rights reserved. No part of this book may be reproduced, stored in a retrieval system or transmitted in any form or by any means—electronic, mechanical, photocopy, recording, or otherwise—without prior written permission of the copyright owner, except by a reviewer who wishes to quote brief passages in connection with a review for inclusion in a magazine, newspaper or broadcast.

Unless otherwise indicated, all Scripture quotations are taken from THE HOLY BIBLE, NEW INTERNATIONAL VERSION®, NIV® Copyright © 1973, 1978, 1984, 2011 by Biblica, Inc.™ Used by permission. All rights reserved worldwide.

DEDICATION

There are so many that we would like to personally thank that it would take another book to contain all their names and still we are sure to miss some very dear and precious saints who have blessed us in our journey.

First, we would like to acknowledge our two daughters, Krista and Tonya, who have persevered through all the changes that have transpired since we were all touched so powerfully in 1995. Krista was 15 and Tonya was 12 years of age and through the past 20 years they have demonstrated God's love and heart for others in a profound way and with a maturity of character that warms our hearts each and every day.

Secondly, we want to thank God for answering the prayers we prayed since our daughters were born, that the men they would marry would be men after God's own heart. We could never have chosen better men for our daughters than Jason for Krista and Josh for Tonya. They are not only Godly men, but have a love and respect for their wives that gives a parent a reason to pause and thank God for His faithfulness in answering our prayers.

Third, we stand in awe at our six grandchildren – Jonah, Simeon, Ezra, Selah, Malakai and Anastasia. We have four boys and two girls, all born within the same span of five years. They are children born out of revival and within them is the course of the destiny of those who have gone before who said 'Yes' to God.

There are those who have supported us in our ministry for years both financially and through their prayers. To Larry and Linda Forster, Lois Peterson, John & Mellie Mackenzie, Ardis Schreiner, Ben and Julie Scofield, and many more, we say from the depths of our heart; thank you, may you receive your reward for your faithfulness and the love you have shown to us both personally and to the ministry.

There are those from Montana who stood by us in prayer, friendship and support from the beginning of the transition in our lives, continuing to this day. We want too especially thank our friends Curt and Janet Konecky, Domenic and Shelly Garefino and Pastors Dan and Karen Sandler.

We are blessed to have a truly anointed editor, Jordan Bateman, who through his encouragement and skill has made this book the blessing it has become. We cannot thank you enough, you make writing a joy and that is a gift from God, and one we do not take lightly.

We would be amiss to not thank Randy and DeAnne Clark, who said yes to God and never looked back. They have made it possible for millions of people to experience the love of our Father in a very real and remarkable way and we will always be grateful to have become a part of their lives as they opened their hearts to us and allowed us to come alongside them in ministry and in friendship and family.

Lastly, we would like to dedicate this book to each other and to the amazing life and memories we have been so blessed to experience together in these past 38 years of marriage. We anticipate the continued adventure for as long as we have breath and for our love to grow even more for one another and for our God as we say "yes" to our Father for all of eternity.

WHEN THE FIRE FALLS

TABLE OF CONTENTS

Chapter	Description	Page
	Dedication	3
	Foreword by Dr. Randy Clark	9
	Endorsements	13
	Introduction	17
1	Let The River Flow	21
2	Spotted Bear	33
3	Pentecost Sunday	41
4	Thursday Night Renewal Meetings	47
5	Youth Retreat At Dickey Lake	55
6	The Early Years	63
7	Jesus Place	73
8	The Journey Continues	81
9	When Creation Comes Alive	89
10	The Night The Lights Went Out	95
11	Taking It To The Streets	99
12	The Goodness Of God	113
13	Doubts And Wonderings	123
14	If It Walks Like A Duck	133
15	Strange Manifestations	145
16	The Anointing	157
	Epilogue	169

WHEN THE FIRE FALLS

FOREWORD

BY DR. RANDY CLARK

When the Fire Falls is an amazing account of the work of the Holy Spirit, written by Rex and Lois Burgher, who are great at telling their story and the story of revival. They deal with so much in the book: power, healing, impartations, deliverance, manifestations, prophecy, words of knowledge, and a general sense of the excitement in the very atmosphere of revival.

I met Rex and Lois Burgher in 1999, and shortly thereafter they were with me on one of my first international trips to Latin America. As I learned about their experiences with God, I was quite intrigued. John Wimber had taught me to pay attention to the people that God's Spirit comes upon in a powerful way. When I heard how God so powerfully touched them that for six months they would wake each other up during the night due to their bodies shaking so hard, I knew to take notice of what God wanted to do with them.

Over time, I developed a closer relationship with Rex and Lois, feeling like God had put them into my life supernaturally. I was impressed with Rex's hunger for God. I was amazed by how he had been healed. His story of giving up a successful construction business where he had several crews working for him spoke volumes to me about his commitment to the Kingdom of God. Eventually, after Rex had traveled on several trips with me (many of which Lois came along on), I asked him if he would like to travel with me as my personal assistant. At first this was on a volunteer basis, but later I hired Rex for this position.

During this season, Rex moved his family to St. Louis where my family lived at the time. We continued to travel the world together, and during the time Rex traveled with me I experienced some of the most powerful meetings in my life. He was with me when I met some of the most powerful ministers in the world. This was a golden time in my itinerate ministry that began in 1994. I connected with Omar Cabrera, Carlos Annacondia, Rolland and Heidi Baker, Leif Hetland, Henry Madava, and many other key leaders around the world.

I loved reading *When the Fire Falls*. It is the kind of book I like to read, biographical, yet with insights, and with details of the activity of the Holy Spirit, including His manifestations. I believe people who are hungry to know more about the ways of the Holy Spirit and His power will both enjoy and learn a lot from *When the Fire Falls*.

When God moved my family from St. Louis to Mechanicsburg, PA, the Burghers came with us, selling their home in St. Louis. Rex was still my personal assistant, and we had many unforgettable experiences together. One other thing Rex and Lois and DeAnne and I have in common are three grandchildren. My oldest son fell in love with his youngest daughter and they married.

For three years, Rex continued to travel with me, until I felt there was nothing more I could teach him. He had heard my teachings so many times he could tell you the next sentence before I said it. I felt it was time for Rex to take the impartation he had received from God, and the knowledge and experience he had gained during those years of assisting me, and begin his own ministry, along with Lois who was in her own right an excellent teacher.

Rex and Lois have their own ministry. I love getting reports from pastors on how the Holy Spirit fell on their congregations when they came and ministered. They are also facilitators for my *Christian Healing Certification Program,* facilitating courses that deal with healing, inner healing, and deliverance. They have been good stewards of what God has entrusted to them.

I want to not only highly recommend *When the Fire Falls* to you as an excellent read, a well-told story told by both Rex and Lois, but I also want to recommend them to you. They have passed the test of time with integrity, humility, continued anointing, and wisdom. Here is a couple that is in pursuit of God, true God chasers, truly laid-down lovers of Jesus.

If you love revival, you will love this book. May you be greatly blessed by the insights, the stories, and the anointing that is on this book. I encourage you to buy *When the Fire Falls,* and I pray it falls on you while reading the book.

Come Holy Spirit – Light the Fire Again!

WHEN THE FIRE FALLS

ENDORSEMENTS

I downloaded the manuscript to *When The Fire Falls*, by Rex and Lois Burgher a few hours ago. I just finished reading it, because--**I couldn't put it down!** A line from the movie Field of Dreams, reminds us that "…We miss the most significant moments of our lives while they are happening to us." This book will produce a longing, a hunger and a desire to either return to a season you once enjoyed, or the desire for one you've always wanted. *When The Fire Falls* is instructive, insightful and inspiring. You will find your appetite whetted for revival and the need to press into the Father's love. I'll read it again.

Bishop Joseph L. Garlington, Sr.
Founding Pastor of Covenant Church of Pittsburgh
Presiding Bishop
Reconciliation! an International Network of Churches and Ministries

Get revived and stay on fire! Do you want to burn brightly without burning out? My friends and authors Rex and Lois have done us all a favor by inviting us on a journey that will help each of us move with focus towards our destiny. This is an invitation for a fresh power and love encounter.

It is also full of wisdom to take you from it being just a

visitation to being a habitation as you learn to live out of God's love not for love.

Leif Hetland
President Global Mission Awareness
Author of 'Seeing Through Heavens Eyes'

Linda and I have known Rex and Lois for over 12 years and have been abundantly blessed by their Godly character, tremendous anointing, and their personal intimacy with God. Their itinerate ministry, Kingdom Life Ministries, brings the Father's heart, healing, deliverance, and the presence of the Holy Spirit wherever they minister. They have chosen abiding in His love and intimacy with our Father first before stressing ministry gifts. The essence of their ministry is reflected in this book.

This book contains the story of Rex and Lois's personal journey into the heart of revival with all of its manifestations, unpredictability, power, and the legacy of changed lives—as told in both a chronological and topical format and within a Biblical, historical, and present day context. Their personal story, writ large, is informative, inspirational, and life changing; and it facilitates the embers of revival to be stoked hot and ready to break out again.

When The Fire Falls is for everyone hungering for more of God, seeking a greater manifestation of the Holy Spirit, and acquiring an enlarged vision of what God is doing in the world. It is well written, easy to absorb, and worth many re-readings to get out of it all it has to offer. It is a must read and sure to fan into flame the heart's desire to personally experience a God led Holy Spirit Revival.

Larry Forster
Colonel, US Army Retired

From all walks of life, each one of us carries the capacity to know the God of the supernatural. In their new book, Rex and Lois Burgher share from their life-changing experiences of encountering God and witnessing amazing moments of Holy Spirit revival. Their story chronicles with transparency a lifestyle of learning to walk with God through the extraordinary and the unknown. Read on and receive more of the Spirit's fire!

Dr. Ché Ahn
Founding Pastor, HROCK Church, Pasadena, CA
President, Harvest International Ministry
International Chancellor, Wagner Leadership Institute

WHEN THE FIRE FALLS

INTRODUCTION

THIS IS OUR STORY

For years, we have wanted to tell our adventure with God. Everything that took place affected us individually, as a couple, and as a family. To be a part of such a glorious and powerful visitation of God is a privilege we hold dear to our hearts.

Our journey allowed us to share in some incredible mountaintop moments, but we also experienced times of great sorrow and frustration. There may be those who read this that were in the same meetings but had experienced something entirely different. We understand how that can happen and respect you for what you experienced, but this is what we saw and felt. It is an accurate portrayal of the truth, as we experienced it. We pray this book gives God all the glory and honor that is due his Holy name and creates in every reader a desire for 'More of God.'

From the first time we read in the book of Acts about what happened when the 'fire fell,' our hearts longed to experience a visitation of His presence. It was not long into our Christian walk that we were given a book about the Azusa Street Revival, the beginning of the modern day Pentecostal movement. To know that times of refreshing still came upon the church was exhilarating and, from that moment, we longed to be a part of one. The seed planted in us at that time came to fruition, and we found ourselves in the midst of a mighty move of His presence. Our dream came true.

We did not begin our Christian walk as Pentecostals, or even as charismatics, but most definitely as people who desired more of God. When the fire of God's presence fell upon our family, we questioned everything that happened to us and read as much as we could on the subject. We journeyed to meetings to listen and watch, asked questions and searched the scriptures to see if this was a legitimate move of the Holy Spirit.

In that search, we found a book called *The History of American Revivals,* which included an account by Rev. Barton W. Stone, a Presbyterian minister. Stone traveled across Kentucky in the spring of 1801 to attend a camp meeting, to see for himself the marvelous things that God had wrought. His story foretells our heart in sharing our own experience:

> *There, on the edge of a prairie in Logan County, Ky., the multitudes came together and continued a number of days and nights encamped on the ground, during which time worship was carried on in some part of the encampment. The scene was new to me and passing strange. It baffled description. Many, very many, fell down as men slain in battle, and continued for hours together in an apparently breathless and motionless state, sometimes for a few moments reviving and exhibiting symptoms of life by a deep groan or piercing shriek, or by a prayer for mercy fervently uttered. After lying for hours, they obtained deliverance. The gloomy cloud that had covered their faces seemed gradually and visibly to disappear, and hope, in smiles, brightened into joy. They would rise, shouting deliverance, and then would address the surrounding multitude in*

language truly eloquent and impressive. With astonishment did I hear men, women, and children declaring the wonderful works of God and the glorious mysteries of the gospel. Their appeals were solemn, heart penetrating, bold, and free. Under such circumstances, many others would fall down into the same state from which the speakers had just been delivered.

Two or three of my particular acquaintances from a distance were struck down. I sat patiently by one of them, whom I knew to be a careless sinner, for hours, and observed with critical attention everything that passed, from the beginning to the end. I noticed the momentary reviving's as from death, the humble confession of sins, the fervent prayer, and the ultimate deliverance; then the solemn thanks to God, and affectionate exhortation to companions and to the people around to repent and come to Jesus. I was astonished at the knowledge of gospel truth displayed in the address. The effect was that several sank down into the same appearance of death. After attending to many such cases, my conviction was complete that it was a good work – the work of God; nor has my mind wavered since on the subject. Much did I see then, and much have I seen since, that I consider to be fanaticism; but this should not condemn the work. The devil has always tried to ape the works of God, to bring them into disrepute; but that cannot be a Satanic work which brings men to humble confession, to forsaking sin, to prayer, fervent praise and thanksgiving, and to a sincere and affectionate exhortation to sinners to repent and come to Jesus the Savior.

- from *The History of American Revivals* by Frank G. Beardsley (pages 91-93)

This is our story, our attempt to describe the supernatural events that we experienced. There were times the noise from the congregation was so loud as the Holy Spirit moved upon people that a person could not hear the speaker, no matter how loud the technicians turned up the volume. People shook, cried, laughed, vibrated and swayed as the Holy Spirit passed over them. Such is the scene we will try to paint for you. If you have experienced a similar move, we pray you will hunger and thirst for those times to return. If you have not, we ask God to birth a desire in you to experience His presence as He moves upon His people.

Experiencing a visitation of the Holy Spirit will explode your senses as you witness the inexplicable entrance of the King of Kings into your midst.

Chapter 1

LET THE RIVER FLOW

May 1995, Kelowna, Canada

"If you are dry and thirsty and need a fresh touch from God, come forward."

The altar call was simple. Within moments, our family was at the front assuming the position that every Vineyard church attendee knows when it comes to receiving prayer. We extended our hands out in front of us, quieted our hearts and waited on God. But we were quickly distracted by a loud, rustling noise behind us. Looking back, we saw what we would later jokingly refer to as the first manifestation of a meeting of this sort - the seemingly unbelievable feat of moving and stacking 1,000 chairs off to the sides of the building in a manner of minutes. At the time, we didn't understand the reason why this was done. Soon it would make perfect sense.

We turned back toward the front and again quieted our hearts. I (Rex) could feel my right hand begin to quiver as the power of God came upon me. Soon two men I had never seen before prayed for me – I looked at them, felt comfortable with them, and closed my eyes to receive.

I fell over. I didn't know why. In the beginning, I had no theology as to why anyone would fall; I just assumed that people fell simply because they could not stand. That day in Kelowna, Canada, I had no experience to guide me. I didn't know why I fell; I had never fallen before nor had I ever felt I would. It was something I had never thought about.

The church was better prepared than I was. They had a person behind me, designated to catch and lower me to the floor. One moment I was standing, hands open to receive – the next, I was laying on the floor.

I didn't know what to do. When I was first saved, no one gave me a manual on what to expect if I found myself on a church floor, so I had to figure everything out for myself. As I laid there, different thoughts came to mind: "Just how long am I supposed to lay here?" Around me, I could sense the other 1,000 attendees milling about. Some of them felt awfully close to me, which prompted another thought: "I hope nobody kicks me in the head, because if someone kicks me in the head, I'm getting up."

My hand began to shake again. "Well, at least that hand shaky thing is happening," I told myself. But should I get up. "How long am I supposed to lie on the floor anyway?"

All these thoughts and more went through my mind; I did not hear any bells nor have any angelic visitations nor see profound visions of the future. I didn't have any great inkling that something was happening to me while I was lying on the floor. No great influx of scriptures came to my mind. But I was not alarmed that I had fallen. Just the opposite, in fact. I felt peaceful. I didn't know it, but my life – and the lives of my wife and children – were being changed in that moment.

Lois laid next to me and went through her own personal transformation. Her experience, though different from mine, was processed through years of church attendance. Oddly, my experience may have been easier since I had no church etiquette to work through; I knew it was God, even with my limited experience with the Holy Spirit.

As I (Lois) laid on the floor, I found myself asking the Lord, "Is this really you? Why have Rex and I fallen on the floor? What is happening?" But another thought overpowered those: "I know the Holy Spirit's presence and the worship brought in the Holy Spirit so powerfully – this must be God!" With that confession, incredible peace came over me. I opened my eyes and saw a beautiful young woman with long red hair sitting beside me and praying that the Holy Spirit would bless and fill me. She ministered to me for over an hour.

As she prayed and I experienced the love of the Father, I received an incredible vision. This experience transformed my heart and my life to such a degree that I have never been the same. In the vision, I found myself on a beautiful mountain meadow being held by our Lord. As He danced with me, I could feel every part of my spirit, mind and heart being filled with the reassurance of His steadfast, faithful and unfathomable love. For the first time in my life, I knew without a shadow of a doubt that He had a love that He had set aside for me, an unquenchable love and fire that no one could take from me because I was truly His beloved bride. When I got up from this transforming experience of being baptized in His love, I had no doubt the Holy Spirit had been at work. The

Lord was preparing my heart for the radical adventure and changes He had planned for our family.

I (Rex) don't know how long Lois and I laid on the floor but I decided to get to my feet. As I rose, I was instantly aware of a tremendous overwhelming transformation that was taking place within me. I felt something happening inside and around me. In the few seconds that it took for me to get up, I felt like I entered a different realm of reality. The change was as startling as if I had suddenly found myself submerged in a pool of water, as intense as passing from one physical reality into another. I was overwhelmed and shocked but also found myself completely saturated by an incredible peace. It was as if I opened my eyes under water and found myself moving in slow motion. Slowly, I became aware of the difference in my surroundings.

As I stood there with the glory of God resting upon me, I tried to speak – and something extraordinary came out. I felt a rushing, gurgling brook of power that bubbled up from my belly and out through my lips. No words came forth – just a gurgling rush of power. I can only describe it like this: in summer, when you turn on a garden hose that has been lying out in the hot sun, you may notice it contains pockets of both water and air. When the water begins to move through the hose, it pushes those pockets of air and water along. Out of the hose comes water, then air, then water, then air, and then finally the full stream of cold water.

It was as if air and water were coming out of me. I could actually feel and see the moisture, like a mist, coming out of my mouth when I tried to speak. When I tried to communicate with those around me, they would immediately collapse to the floor. I wasn't frightened, because of the incredible peace of God that I felt, but I just couldn't get anyone to help me understand what was happening to me. As the power intensified, I couldn't go near anyone without them falling. Soon, anyone who was within twenty feet of me was on the floor, out under the power of God.

The two men who had first prayed for me came back and said, "There is something very significant that has taken place within you and we release you to go and pray for others." At the time, I didn't think it was strange that they would come back and release me to pray for people. However, as the months went by and we grew close to several of the people on the prayer team, we discovered none of them knew the two men who had prayed for us that day. We also found out it was forbidden to have anyone other than prayer team members pray for people. I never saw those two men again; whoever they were, they affected our lives forever.

As Lois laid peacefully upon the floor, I moved as if in slow motion, making gurgling sounds and watching people fall. Some laughed uncontrollably or wept. Some shook like pieces of bacon on a hot griddle while others laid there peacefully. It was a surreal scene. Looking around, I found our oldest daughter, 15-year-old Krista, as she got up from the floor. It appeared as if she was being forcefully bent over and then jerking back up. This happened again and again as she walked across the floor. Every time she tried to stop these jerks from happening, she would begin to speak in a Chinese type of language. It was either one or the other: speak in this strange dialect or close her mouth and begin jerking. This was completely out of our realm of experience – none of us had ever spoken in tongues. For more than a week after our return to Montana, this strange behavior continued.

I stood, gurgled and looked at Lois and Krista. Everyone

around us seemed to be experiencing bizarre things as well. It was all more than I could comprehend; my senses overloaded. As I tried to get my bearings, an Asian woman came and asked me in broken English, "Could your daughter pray for my daughter?" She pointed to a young girl lying on the floor twenty feet away. "My daughter not speaks English, but your daughter speaks our language so well!" I nodded and watched her lead Krista over to her daughter. For more than half an hour, Krista talked with the girl laying on the floor – in her own language. This was a language Krista never learned nor heard before but was given through the Holy Spirit. She told me later that as they talked she could see the words form in her mind and she knew immediately what the girl was saying. She just answered her.

Our youngest daughter, 12-year-old Tonya, was deeply touched in those meetings too. She was moved like a deep current under the sea. For months after, she would be found weeping in her room. I would ask her what was wrong and she would look into my eyes and say, "Who is going to save them, Dad? Who is going to tell them?" To this day, I can see within her God's immeasurable love for lost humanity.

For the next three days and nights, the four of us were lost in God's presence. Being under the influence of the Holy Spirit became a way of life as we took in the goodness of God, along with the bewilderment of all that happened around us. We had never seen anything like those meetings. Often the sounds of people being touched by God would drown out the preaching in the room.

We were so powerfully touched by God that we would fall asleep at night only to be awakened at all hours by our bodies trembling under His anointing and power. The Holy Spirit would gently nudge one of us awake and whispering the most holy name of Jesus would start us shaking. The other would wake too, and the shaking would continue for both of us under His power. Months later, we wondered if we would ever get a real night's sleep again as the Holy Spirit continued to awaken us with His touch. Awake or asleep, God had captured us. There were very few moments that His presence could not be tangibly felt; we found ourselves continually overwhelmed.

We saw manifestations of the power of God that we never imagined or believed possible. One man, sitting in a chair, rocked back and forth with such force that his forehead would come within a foot of the floor in front and his hair would almost touch the floor behind him. Never once did he lose his balance, nor did it appear as if he was out of control.

At times, Lois and I would walk around the sanctuary and just watch what God was doing. Once, we went upstairs to the balcony, which completely circled the sanctuary. As we gazed down, we were amazed at how people were affected when the Holy Spirit came upon them. We saw a third of them sway this way and that, like wheat in a field when the wind blows. No one could orchestrate that kind of synchronized movement. Some laughed uncontrollably; we watched as others would turn to them and in frustration tell them to be quiet, only to find themselves begin to laugh uncontrollably. Some shook quite violently for long periods of time, while others would sporadically tremble. Some shot out their arms or legs in strange directions, shaking uncontrollably. Others jerked like Krista, while some had their hands and arms jerk up and down at the oddest of times. It was like an invisible conductor orchestrated the whole thing – lifting his baton and directing each person with a precision that was a wonder to watch.

At the end of one of the worship sessions, we all remained silently standing and soaking in the glory of the Lord. Across the room, a man demonically manifested. He screamed out in a snarled demonic voice that could not have been his, "I hate you, I hate you all!" His arms were above his head and his hands were twisted and bent in an unnatural and grotesque manner. One of the speakers ran to the edge of the platform, jumped to the floor and ministered to the man. Sitting on his chair, waiting to speak, Vineyard founder John Wimber smiled and took the microphone. "Isn't this great? This man who was bound is now going to be set free," John said. The man was taken to another room, set free, returned to the meeting and was a different person during the rest of the conference.

After one afternoon session, we saw a bizarre manifestation, one we never saw again. We counted seven women, each of them taking approximately twenty square foot of space on the floor, violently thrown from side to side, much like a fish thrashes when out of the water. It was not graceful. Their sleeves tore and rug burns formed on their arms and knees as they flopped. Lois and I watched them, and I told her I felt a peace about it all. She looked at me and said, "What could you possibly find peaceful about any of this?" As I looked again at the women on the floor, I said, "I guess I find some peace in the fact it's only happening to women and not men."

We had come to Kelowna not realizing the meetings were part of the outpouring that had started some time before in Toronto. We had read about Toronto in *Charisma Magazine*, but never connected it with Kelowna or John Wimber, who we had previously seen in 1986 in Columbia, South Carolina. We did know that John was battling a cancer he was not expected to recover from, and we wanted to see him again and have our daughters experience his ministry. Coming to hear John and the amazing Vineyard worship disguised our true purpose for being there. We were in a dry place spiritually and needed a fresh touch from God. We came to the meeting, listened to the first night's message and worshipped in song but not with complete abandon. We certainly did not dance. However, when the Holy Spirit came, we danced so hard our legs ached all night long. Our voices became hoarse from singing with everything within us. We had never experienced such a time of celebration in Jesus, but now we were in love and we wanted the whole world to know.

As we drove home, we passed people on the road from the conference with signs taped to their car windows that said, "More Lord!" Just seeing those words sent us into spasms as our bodies would jerk uncontrollably. Such power, such love!

As we approached the outskirts of Spokane, Washington, we saw a young, scantily clad woman hitchhiking. She looked hardened, desperate and alone. In an instant, I (Lois), heard the Holy Spirit confirming within me that she was a prostitute. I felt an incredible sadness and remorse over her condition. I was overwhelmed with the love of God as my heart was filled with the compassion that our Lord has for her. I sobbed uncontrollably and prayed intensely for her soul. A week earlier, I would have been disgusted by this woman; now it took several minutes for me to overcome my emotions and explain to Rex and the girls why I was weeping for her.

I knew then I had been transformed to see and feel differently. Our Lord loves with an unconditional love that surpasses all human understanding and He has complete compassion on the broken ones, He came to bring freedom to the captives. Isaiah 61:1 took on a fresh revelation as I discovered how He wanted us to be His ambassadors in a broken and dying world: *"The Spirit of the Sovereign Lord is on me, because the Lord has anointed me to proclaim good news to the poor. He has sent me to bind up the brokenhearted, to proclaim freedom for the captives and release from darkness for the prisoners."*

After a ten-hour drive, we arrived home in Kalispell, Montana, late Sunday night, exhausted. Our sleep was what we had come to expect; we trembled under the power of God. We awakened the next morning to begin something that was far beyond our wildest dreams.

TUESDAY NIGHT – THE SECOND NIGHT HOME

Forty-eight hours after getting home, it was our turn to host the weekly cell group with several members of the pastoral staff, church elders, and their wives. Coincidentally, our pastor had just returned from the annual Christian and Missionary Alliance meeting, held in Pittsburgh that year. The evening started like it always did; we chatted about the church, an elder led us in worship, and our pastor talked about the Pittsburgh meeting. Finally, he turned to us and asked about Kelowna.

We could barely contain ourselves. We told them what we had seen and experienced, and started praying for them. The most interesting thing happened: all the women in the room fell backwards, and all the men fell face forward. Our pastor started mumbling loudly – we had to wait until he lifted his face from the carpet before we could hear him say: "Okay, You're God and I'm not." All of a sudden, he flipped over onto his back and laughed and laughed. Quickly, the other men flipped too and howled with laughter. Our pastor later told us he had been determined that he was not going to fall down, no matter what. We found that odd, as falling over hadn't been part of our church's normal experience. In fact, we had never seen it happen, although a few others could recall the odd occurrence.

THURSDAY NIGHT – THE FOURTH NIGHT HOME

On Thursday night, I (Rex) decided to attend the church's designated weekly prayer meeting. At the time, the meeting was lucky to draw a dozen people of our 350 church attendees. It was hot in the church that evening, and I sat and watched everything. Near the end, our pastor asked me to come forward and share. I stood to my feet and told what was happening to me personally, but did not go into the wild things we had witnessed in Kelowna.

That was the last calm prayer meeting we had for almost a year. On Pentecost Sunday, 1995, all Heaven broke loose. When the next Thursday rolled around, the prayer meeting was packed with more than 250 people.

WHEN THE FIRE FALLS

Chapter 2

SPOTTED BEAR

NEAR GLACIER PARK, MONTANA

The first weekend after Kelowna, my pastor convinced me (Rex) to come to a weekend men's retreat at the Spotted Bear Ranch, located 60 miles down a gravel road between Glacier Park and the Bob Marshall Wilderness. It was an outdoorsman's paradise, and the retreat drew more than 60 men with the promise of fishing and hiking. Some Bible study and prayer time were also planned, but most had signed up for the recreation – did I mention the fishing? Like most men's retreats, the focus of the men was not so much on the Creator as it was on getting out and enjoying His Creation. None of us could have imagined what God had in store.

It took more than two hours to get there, and we were late. I found my assigned cabin, left my stuff on my bunk and went straight for dinner. Most of the men had already arrived and, after a quick bite, we all filed into the main area of the lodge. The head of our men's fellowship started off with some guidelines for the weekend, going over the schedule, and running down a list of available activities. A good Bible study followed, but the men sat through it as if it was the last day of school and the only thing between them and a summer of fun was getting through that next hour.

Probably the biggest schoolchild was our pastor, who sat right beside me. He kept nudging me saying, "Let's start praying for everyone." After a few nudges, I told him, "Look, you're the pastor, you go ahead and interrupt him." Fortunately, the study wrapped up and he jumped to his feet. "Let's pray for people," he said. Almost immediately, a young man that I did not recognize raised his hand and sprang to his feet. We prayed for five full minutes without seeing so much as a twitch of his eye. I did not know what to do; I was so new to this that all I knew to do was to keep on praying. I was relieved when our pastor, who knew the man, told him to sit down. The pastor told me later that God had revealed to him that the enemy had sent him to stop what was about to happen. As soon as the next man came forward and stood before us, the power of God came upon him so hard and fast that he crumbled to the ground. He cried out in such anguish we thought for sure he must be in incredible pain. However, as quickly as he screamed out in agony, he stopped, and after audibly sighing, he became completely restful. Then without warning, he grabbed his stomach, doubled up and rolled over on the floor, letting out another cry of anguish. We would just start to react and he would go back to lying peacefully.

The floodgates of Heaven opened and men all over the room experienced the sovereign outpouring of God's favor. We prayed as fast as any two people could pray but God often met the men before we even got a chance to pray for them.

All the while, the noise level increased with men falling to the floor as they became overwhelmed in the spirit. Many laughed uncontrollably while others lay quietly. The first man was still periodically screaming out in pain. Not knowing what to do with him, I decided to get a couple of men to carry him out to a padded bench in an adjoining room. There, he was out of the way and God could continue to do whatever it was He was doing. Later, I noticed another man had gone over and sat on the floor next to him. The second man laughed uncontrollably; waves of laughter would come out from so deep within him, it caused him to grab his stomach every time another bout would come. You could almost see it start in his stomach and roll up and out of him.

Not everyone in the room was comfortable with what was happening. One man asked if I was going to continue to let this go on. I understood his concern; I knew it was a wild scene. If I had not just come from a week of it myself, I would have thought it very strange. I asked him if there was anything in particular he was worried about. Even as I said it, I realized how foolish that sounded – all I had to do was look around at everything that was happening in the room.

He pointed to the man we had carried over to the bench and the other man who sat on the floor beside him. "How long are you going to allow that man sitting on the floor to laugh at that other man who is in such obvious pain?" he asked. His question was as ludicrous as my wondering which part of the evening was strange to him. He thought the man sitting on the floor was laughing hysterically at someone writhing in pain.

I checked on the man who was crying out. As I approached him, he let out another of his painful cries, clutching his stomach. As it subsided, I asked him if he was all right. He opened his eyes and, looking straight into mine, said, "I am experiencing the most incredible peace of the Lord that I have ever felt." His eyes closed, and he screamed out again. I turned back to where the concerned man was waiting for me. I realized that I really knew nothing of what God was doing in our midst. "He says he's experiencing the peace of the Lord," I told him. "Oh good, I was really concerned," the man replied, turning and casually walking away.

Later, I learned the man who cried out in agony had been in two major car accidents and was in such bad physical condition that he could hardly walk across a room without feeling a tremendous amount of pain. When he told his doctor that he was going to a men's retreat near Glacier Park, he was advised not to go. The next morning, he awoke from where we left him on the couch without any pain and joined a group of men on a five-mile hike. He had no problem keeping up with them and from that moment on experienced no pain at all.

As I moved around the room, I prayed for a man when the most incredible unction from God came upon me. With an intense tone in my voice, I told everyone to get back. I almost physically shoved three men who were near me because I knew something was coming and coming fast! Suddenly the Holy Spirit came in such power that all of us were physically propelled backward. The man shuddered violently from the top of his head down to the soles of his feet and crashed to the ground. It was as if he was in a powerful downdraft of the Holy Spirit, causing every fiber of his being to vibrate. We all looked at each other and knew we had witnessed an incredible sight. At the same time, I felt the most incredible, tangible presence of holiness that I had ever experienced before. Silence gripped us. We knew we were on holy ground. We left him there in that place of silence, and many of us noticed that the sounds in the room would dim whenever we came near that young man.

As I looked around the room, I was amazed. I was

impressed by how the men had begun to pray for one another. The supernatural firestorm was still intensely burning. Every now and then, a flare of God's presence would swoop down upon the men and the noise of yells, laughter, crying, jerking and falling filled the air. In those moments, I could hardly hear someone talking right next to me. It was almost more than the senses could take in, but there seemed to be a sense of peaceful order in the chaos.

Hours passed. It was well after midnight when we staggered back to our cabins. Many of us were so filled by God's goodness that we found it difficult to walk in a straight line. Our worship pastor was so overwhelmed by the Holy Spirit that I had to help him as he laughed uncontrollably all the way back to the cabin. More than once I held him upright as he laughed so hard he sank to the ground. We finally arrived at the cabin and got into our bunks. My last thought as I fell asleep listening to him laugh was wondering how smart it was to put him on the top bunk, especially in his condition.

I had just drifted off to sleep when suddenly the worship pastor thumped to the floor next to me, laughing uncontrollably. It was apparent from his rolling around the floor in a fit of laughter that he was all right. My pastor, with just a look, pleaded for me to do something. It was not yet daybreak, but I knew it was useless to try and get him back up to his bunk so I took him out in the brisk, early morning air, put him in my pickup truck, and turned on Brian Doerksen's *Light The Fire Again* tape. For more than two hours, we sat in that pickup as the presence of God lifted us higher into His presence. It seemed like time stood still as the glory of God continually rolled over us, so thick that we felt we were in the very presence of God. It was one of the most incredible and intimate times I had ever experienced with God.

A few hours later, we decided to go over for breakfast and prayer before everyone disappeared into the woods for the day. Getting out of the pickup was easy but we soon found that both of us were having difficulty walking. We stumbled along under the influence of the Holy Spirit, and eventually made it up the steps of the main lodge. Going through the main door, we discovered we were too late for breakfast but we could hear the final instructions being given to the men in the main room. Swaying back and forth, and trying not to fall, we kept trying to stifle the laughter that was bubbling up within us. Using the walls for support, we slid our way down to where we could peek around the corner and into the room. As soon as we looked around the corner, laughter erupted from us both and we quickly ducked back out of sight to try and keep our composure.

The meeting ended, but we continued to lean against the wall. The men filed past us and out of the room. Without any explanation, I got the impression from God that He wanted me to pray for four of the men that were passing by. As they came near me, I stopped them and asked if they would mind staying for a second. Once everyone else had left, I turned to the four remaining men and our pastors and told them that God had impressed upon me to ask if I could pray for them. Without exception, they agreed. I didn't find out until later that those four men had approached the pastor at breakfast complaining about everything that had happened the night before. After hearing how they had complained, it is amazing they stayed at the retreat or even agreed to receive prayer.

I didn't know any of that. I went to the first man and watched as he immediately fell to the floor. I hadn't even raised my hand, much less had the opportunity to say anything to him. I turned to pray for the next man and he also dropped to the floor. Just as quickly, the last two men joined them. With all four of them now on the floor, the first man yelled for help. He was not panicked, but laughed as he informed us that his butt was stuck to the floor and he could not get up. He tried turning and twisting, doing everything he could to get up, but he just could not seem to get unstuck. He looked intoxicated in God's presence. His hair was a mess, his face was red from laughter, and the exertion he was making trying to get up made for a funny sight.

The second man told us his head felt glued to the floor. We watched as he twirled around in a circle with his head seemingly glued in one place. Each of them had a separate and unique experience with God that day. However we found out later that having a great experience is not enough to change a person; you have to walk out your time of visitation as well.

Feeling released by the Holy Spirit to discontinue praying, I left them basking in the presence of the Lord and went into the dining hall. Finding the pastors sitting at a table waiting for me, we headed outside to enjoy the sunshine along with the incredible mountain scenery, before the lunch bell would ring. The presence of God was so real and tangible that it felt like we were wading chest deep through a flowing stream of the glory of God. Heady with the presence of God, we headed down a trail and came to a swaying bridge that was suspended at least fifty feet above a rushing stream. Hanging on to side ropes, we made it across and down the trail a short distance until the humidity along the stream and a swarm of mosquitoes convinced us to go back to the bridge.

We made it to the middle of the bridge when God suddenly surprised us and we all collapsed, laughing hysterically. For more than an hour, we swayed back and forth over the rushing stream, rolling and laughing uncontrollably. We laughed even harder as our senior pastor tried to have a complicated theological discussion with another man who had finally made it out to where we were. His questions seemed so absurd to us that with each one we laughed until our sides hurt.

God had mercy on us and we were able to make it back to our feet with each other's assistance. We finished our journey across the bridge, back to the safety of land. As we did, another friend arrived. He had missed the previous night and breakfast, but as soon as he saw us, the power of God overwhelmed him. The spirit of God was so strongly on him that we thought we would need to send someone to help him. We were surprised to look back and see him lunge from one tree to the next, holding on just long enough to propel himself up the trail.

At lunch, we told the men that much of the leadership team had to miss the evening meeting in order to get back and prepare for church Sunday morning. They were visibly disappointed, as they had been looking forward to the evening with great expectations for a touch from God. Without hesitation, I explained that it was not us, but God who was using us. He would use them in the same way.

After they returned, one of the men told me that evening was one of the most powerful times of his life. Our leaving was designed by God, and He used this time to allow others to move in an anointing they previously did not know was available to them.

Chapter 3

PENTECOST SUNDAY

The Day the Fire Fell

Sunday morning was the seventh day back from Kelowna and already so much had happened that it was mind boggling to put the divine sequence of events together. I (Rex) returned home from the men's retreat early enough Saturday night to get a good night's sleep, and awoke Sunday ready for church.

Not long before, our church had outgrown our building and added a second service. We hurried to get to church for the first service. Except for the two pastors and me, none of the other men had returned from Spotted Bear, so no one knew what had happened at the retreat. The service began like normal, with only one unusual difference: it was full. When our pastor came forward after worship, he did something he had never done before, and said, simply, "If you are dry and thirsty and want a fresh touch from God, please come forward."

Those words sparked a stampede and more than 150 people streamed forward. God had prepared our congregation for what was about to happen, and predestined that it was our time of visitation. Finding us in the middle of the tightly-packed sea of people looking for something more from God, our pastor said,

"Rex and Lois, start praying for people."

We looked around and spotted the church's youth leaders. Motioning for them to follow us, we went up the steps onto the platform, which was the only place that had any space for us to pray for them. They followed us, found some room and, as they turned around to face us, they both went out in the spirit and melted to the floor. We didn't even get a chance to pray or say anything to them; we had not touched them or even raised our hands.

Stunned, we turned around to see two elderly women following us up the steps to receive prayer. They were almost up the three steps to the platform when they froze. Their eyes widened when they saw what happened to the youth pastors. Bewildered, they looked at us, and tried as fast as they could to back down the steps from where they had just come. They stepped backwards down the steps to the floor. You could see they were trying to get their minds wrapped around what just happened when suddenly the power of God came upon them and they too melted to the floor.

We walked along the edge of the platform, parallel to the people standing below, and watched as the power of God came. As we walked past, people would fall to the floor, overwhelmed by the Holy Spirit, without anyone touching them. Some we did actually get to lay hands on, but many just fell under the glory. Unlike Kelowna, our church did not have catchers – it just was not part of our culture and it wouldn't have done us any good anyway as the crowd was so tightly packed that there was only space to slide down the mass of people and onto the floor. Some became catchers out of reflex as people toppled onto them. Within minutes, the place was a sea of sounds as the Holy Spirit laid out upon the floor those who had been touched.

At one point, I looked at the back of the church and saw a group of 40 people that I did not recognize. They crowded against the back wall, talking amongst themselves and pointing towards the front. Later, we learned they were a group of former Baptists who had recently left their Baptist church to attend a charismatic church - only to find their leaders had gone to Toronto to "catch the fire" and bring it back to their fellowship. The blessing did not come back to the church from Toronto, but they were so upset that the leaders would even think of going they all left the church anyway. It just happened that the first church they decided to visit was ours. They ran right into the same thing they had run away from.

Soon the floor of the church was packed with people laying everywhere. Bodies continued up the aisles toward the back of the sanctuary. Before we knew it, the first service quickly turned into the second service as people began to crowd into the sanctuary for what was normally the start of church. But no one from the first service was leaving because most of them were still scattered on the floor, unable or unwilling to get up.

I glanced over at the youth pastors. They had made it up off the floor and now sat in the front row under the influence of God. He was laughing so uncontrollably that he was trying to hide his face in his wife's long skirt; she was trying in an un-sober way to get him to stop it and sit up.

The second service was a continuance of the first and renewal was officially birthed within our church. Several weeks later, we realized that the Sunday it all began was Pentecost

Sunday. That service was one of the most powerful times we had witnessed. To see so many people overwhelmed by the power of God was a blessing. Our pastor used the same phrase that we had heard in Kelowna, the same words that drew us to the front for prayer. I know that we never told him about it, but out of his mouth came the words, "If you are dry and thirsty and want a fresh touch from God please come forward." And they did!

For the next year, every Thursday night was renewal night. On those nights, we would go upstairs and pray for the fire of God to come in the meeting. Since the church had formed a prayer ministry team, we would pray for the team of about twenty people. There were many times in our preparation for the meetings that the Holy Spirit would overtake us and we would barely be able to move downstairs to go to the service itself.

The Baptists standing along the back wall were not the only ones who were unhappy about what was happening. As the weeks and months came and went, others either left the church or stayed and caused confusion by spreading mistruths. We spent hours meeting with people and talking to them about our experiences. Some listened, but others simply were not comfortable with what was going on. We were not comfortable with everything that was taking place either, but we decided it was better to try and tame a wild horse, rather than resurrect a dead one. With all the problems associated with revival we determined that the presence of God coming in power, though not fully understood, was well worth the challenges it seemed to cause.

Eight people from our church went to Kelowna and experienced, to some extent, what we had. Each of them came home and had to process what they had seen and experienced.

Some embraced what was happening while trying to make sense of it. Others watched to see how people reacted to it; when some they respected seemed hesitant, they backed off and later became opponents of it. For some it became the best of times; for others, it was the worst of times. For us, it was the beginning of how the Lord would bless and change the rest of our lives.

WHEN THE FIRE FALLS

Chapter 4

THURSDAY NIGHT RENEWAL MEETINGS

Kalispell, Montana

The church was packed the first Thursday night after our Pentecost Sunday breakthrough – more than 250 people crowded in. They were there for all kinds of reasons: some came out of a hunger for God, others out of curiosity, and still others were simply drawn by the spiritual activity that promised to happen. Some of these people were just plain strange; this is a common phenomenon when God moves. Within the first month of the outpouring, we seemed to attract every unique person that had attended any church within a 200-mile radius, as well as some new age practitioners, occultists, and witches. We put up as many safeguards as possible to stop unknown and questionable people from ministering to anyone, but the fact they were even there caused some Christians to mistrust what was happening. This is a sad statement on the state of the Church. We are so used to the status quo that includes only the presentable, wealthy, and healthy people in our churches that we forget Jesus came to minister to the sick, to the demonically oppressed, to the broken ones – and that they were a part of every meeting Jesus and His disciples held.

BICYCLING IN THE HEAVENLIES

In those early renewal meetings, there was one young woman we found especially interesting. She was thin, timid and usually quiet, but she exhibited a peculiar manifestation. She would fall down almost immediately and lying upon her back, she would start moving her arms and legs as if she were pedaling an upside down bicycle. Once in a while, she would speak out loud bits and pieces of the thoughts that must have been floating around in her mind. We did not stop her, as she was not burdening anyone or doing anything indecent or ungodly, but it seemed odd. Once, I (Rex) was praying a few feet away from her when she called out in a loud voice, "Get the wax off your ears, Rex, get the wax off your ears!" In the moment, I thought she had told me to get the wax *out of* my ears; later, she corrected me that she said, "*Off* your ears, not *out of* your ears." That didn't make it any more understandable.

Of course, we didn't understand much of anything that was happening in those first few months, as the Holy Spirit manifested on people. We just let things go, especially if they appeared to be harmless.

On another night, I was praying for a group of people, across the church from where she was pedaling her imaginary bicycle. It was noisy, as 300 people had jammed the sanctuary, and fully a third of them were experiencing the presence of God as the worship team played. Praying for someone involved yelling just to be heard. A worship leader had prayed with a young man but was not making much headway. Frustrated, he asked me what was stopping the man from getting the breakthrough he so desperately wanted. As I thought, God showed me that the young man had not given his life to Jesus: "Did you ask if he knew the Lord?" I said.

Suddenly, the music lulled and people quieted down. From across the room came the voice of our bicyclist: "That's right, pastor, ask him if he knows the Lord! The Lord! Ask him if he knows the Lord!" We were shocked at the accuracy and timing of her word. There was no way that she could have heard our conversation; we had yelled into each other's ears just to be barely heard. Clearly, this lady was bicycling in a realm we knew very little about.

In the weeks and months to come, she prophesied over me several times. I would usually dismiss the words, but that didn't make them wrong. Once she said she saw me running up and down piles of garbage; another time, she saw me on the Great Wall of China. I had no desire to do any of those things. Frankly, I thought it a waste of money to go outside of the United States on short term ministry trips knowing that there was enough work to do in this country. However, a couple of years later, I found myself walking on piles of garbage with Rolland and Heidi Baker in Mozambique, and I have seen the Great Wall as we flew into Beijing.

When people visit a church, whether it is a regular Sunday morning service or during a move of God, they often judge that church by what they see. All it takes is one peculiar individual to color what those observers think of the entire church or move of God. It's all-too-human to focus on a negative individual experience and make it the overarching storyline for what is happening in a place.

Early in the renewal, we had one girl who, after being on the floor for a while, would scream. At the time, we did not know what to do with her, especially since we had just a basic understanding of how to properly deliver someone. We just let her scream and with all the other sounds in the room, she usually blended in. We talked about it and decided that we would deal with things as the Holy Spirit led. After some time, we realized that none of us had ever heard her give a "healthy" scream, so we decided to get her up off the floor, take her over to the side and find out what was going on. I (Lois) discovered she was an abused and hurt young woman who needed ministry and God's love to heal her brokenness. I remember praying over her many times, asking God to heal her wounds with His love; often, she would receive His peace and quiet down.

Some leaders feel if a revival breaks out in their church, they should hold protracted nightly meetings until it's over. Our church community chose a different path. We felt one day a week worked well for us and it seemed natural that Thursday night would be a good time for renewal. Later the pastor tried to keep the outpouring to Thursday nights and not let it spill over into our Sunday morning services. However, this was nearly impossible unless you manipulated the service in such a way as to stop the Holy Spirit from moving as He wished. I (Lois) remember becoming so overwhelmed with His presence on a Sunday morning that I slipped out of the pew, onto the floor. I spent most of the service under that pew, no matter how hard I tried to get up. It is hard to straddle the fence while in a move of God by trying to balance those that are hungry for more with those who do not want change. Better to embrace the move and see where God leads.

Another woman, who had been going to counseling for years, was powerfully touched and set free by experiencing God's love and total acceptance. She had been transformed and, because of the freedom she had experienced herself, we released her to pray and minister to others. The people she prayed for also experienced His love and freedom. This caused quite a stir among those who had known her for years. How could she now be free and whole enough to minister to others when she had been in bondage and oppression for so long? That's the work of Jesus.

PRE-SERVICE PRAYER

To help minister to all of those who were coming, our pastor formed a prayer team, which at times numbered as many as 35. Before the meetings, we gathered for an hour for pre-service prayer. These were some profound and powerful times, as the Lord gave us prophetic words to build up and encourage one another. We grew close as a team. In the services, our pastor asked the prayer team to line up along the front. Before beginning ministry time, he would have us pray for the team itself. Within a few minutes, all 35 of the ministry team would end up lying upon the floor, touched by the Holy Spirit. Most experienced His presence by shaking, laughing, jerking, or simply being so overwhelmed by Him that they couldn't even stand. This was both good and bad in practical terms. On the good side, the crowd got to see the presence of God come upon the prayer team and their lives were blessed. However, it was hard to assemble the prayer team to pray for others once this happened. Invariably, we lost half our team for the rest of the evening.

After praying for the ministry team, the pastor asked those in the crowd who wanted to receive prayer to come to the front. At times, it was incredibly wild as people experienced the power and presence of God. Since the congregation sat on pews, bolted to the floor, there was no easy way to move them. This made trying to find a place for everyone a problem. It didn't take long before the front and every aisle would overflow; people would even move into the vestry on occasion. We found ministering to people was a lot like being a real estate agent: location, location, location.

One of our early problems was that a couple of people, who were not content in waiting for God to move, decided to help by pushing people down. This prompted the pastor to issue a decree that we not touch anyone as we prayed. If it looked strange before, it looked really bizarre now. With God landing powerfully on the prayer team, their arms would flap, their hands would shake, and sometimes the catchers were not sure who was going to go down first, the pray-ers or the pray-ees. It didn't matter if anyone had a hand touch them or not, just a wave and a spoken word to receive "More, Lord," would impact the person receiving prayer.

For close to a year the Holy Spirit came powerfully to our Thursday night renewal meetings. He transformed and changed us, and we experienced His love and power in a profound outpouring of His increased presence in our lives. Sometimes it was so powerful that you could just walk past people and they would fall out in the spirit. Other times you could come up behind a person and just raise your hand and without them knowing you were even there, they would fall to the floor.

One night we visited some of our oldest friends to eat dinner. We knew that they were not fully in favor of what was happening but it was not our intent to discuss it or defend it – we just wanted to have a nice evening with our friends. However, the conversation quickly turned and the wife made a comment that stuck with us. "I get everything going smoothly in my life, my family, my work and God and every time God comes in power it upsets and changes everything and it takes me a long time to get them back to where I feel comfortable," she said. That's how some people view revival. But everyone needs to come to terms with allowing the Lord to change and mold their life. We each have to make choices with what we do when God visits us powerfully.

For more than twenty years, we have lived in the heart of revival. We have traveled the world and sat with some of the most influential leaders of the revival. Revival is not easy. It can often be a struggle. You may lose some of your closest friends, but you will make other friends. You may end up giving up your home and property, moving to another part of the world or country. Your career could change completely, and your children may end up marrying entirely different people then if you stayed where you were. But it is worth everything. The decisions you make not only affect you, but your children and your children's children. You are changing the destiny of your family for generations. When we say yes to His plans for our lives, we trust Him to know and see far beyond anything we could have dreamed.

WHEN THE FIRE FALLS

Chapter 5

YOUTH RETREAT AT DICKEY LAKE

The Book Of Acts Revisited

The young man was hysterical, flailing and stumbling, as he tried to grab someone near him. "I can't see! I can't see!" he yelled. Others gathered around him and were overcome by his desperation. They cried out too. Soon it was a mass of humanity, feeding on the hysteria of the moment. The Holy Spirit had arrived and was making Himself known in the hearts of those in His presence. God had entered the meeting, and this youth retreat was just beginning to feel His impact.

A couple of days before the retreat, our worship pastor asked if we could come up and pray for the kids. He was in charge of the retreat, which drew youth from several churches in our denomination. The setting was spectacular; the retreat was on the edge of a pristine, beautiful mountain lake. It was a picturesque camp, with rustic cabins, canoes, a beautiful beach, and a dining area that jutted out over the lake. It looked like it came right out of a Thomas Kinkade painting.

We were honored to accept his invitation. Our oldest

daughter Krista had attended the camp for a couple of years and knew most of the kids. They always had a great time and the previous year they had a very powerful time of ministry with several of the girls having open visions of things to come. Just one year later, those 'things to come' started to be fulfilled.

When we arrived, we asked to speak with the key leaders of the camp, including the wife of a local pastor, the guest speaker, and other adults there to supervise. Our pastor brought us all together and we told them what happened to us in Kelowna and what the Lord had been doing when we prayed for people. They assured us they were all right with everything and told us to go for it. We were taken aback by their total acceptance – unfortunately, it didn't last. In our defense, we told them what had been happening when we prayed for people.

The building that served as the sanctuary was old and rustic. Inside were a few pews along with mismatched chairs that had been donated from a variety of people and churches. It really did look like something out of the backwoods. We went to the back of the sanctuary and put our things on some of the seats along the back wall. Since it was early and the kids were still finishing their dinner, we went and laid hands on each of the chairs and prayed for the kids that would soon be sitting there. We finished praying as the kids filed in, so we sat down and watched. We felt the Holy Spirit powerfully on us as we anticipated what He would do that evening.

It was funny to watch the kids during the service. Like the old Sidney Poitier movie, *To Sir, With Love*, these young people could not care less about what the speakers had to say. They were disinterested in everything that was happening around them except having a good time with each other. As I wondered about how any of this was going to work, I lifted my hand slightly and, moving it to cover the back of the head of each youth, I prayed that God would touch them powerfully.

To say the antics of the kids were comical is an understatement. Not only were they bored with what was happening, a couple of them were making out in front of us. One dark-haired teenager seemed to be the "cool" kid; his only interest was in the young girl beside him. The main speaker did a good job, but the majority of the kids showed no response to anything he had to say. He just did not seem to be connecting with them. After a while he finished and gave a passionate altar call. We watched as no one moved.

After ten minutes of sincere calls, which turned into pleas for anyone to come to the altar, the speaker sat down and covered his face with his hands. We had been asked to come and pray for the kids but there didn't seem to be anyone to be prayed for. Then, as the music quieted down, our worship pastor asked us to come forward.

We walked past the speaker, who still had his face buried in his hands. With Lois beside me, I closed my eyes and prayed into the microphone. I chose my words carefully and spoke softly and slowly. "I ask the Holy Spirit to come, the same Spirit that came on the day of Pentecost, the same Spirit that lighted upon Jesus as a dove when He was baptized, the One promised by Jesus to all who believe," I said. A noise rose up among the kids and became a deafening roar. It was like the floodgates of Heaven opened and God poured out His power upon us. I opened my eyes to a scene that was incredible to behold. Kids all over the place were crying and holding onto one another. Some laughed, while others slumped in their pews holding on as if the ground was a powerful magnet pulling them down.

The noise was deafening and the scene surreal. We went as fast as we could, from one person to the next, praying as the Lord led us. That's when the young man became hysterical and yelled out, "I can't see! I can't see!" As other kids gathered around him, they cried too, feeding on the hysteria of the moment. I (Lois) went to him and calmly moved him away from the others, sat him down, and prayed for him. He was terrified, but he finally settled down enough that he could answer my questions. After a half an hour of asking the young man questions, I finally received a word from the Lord as to the reason for his loss of vision.

"Are you involved in pornography?" I asked. Even the bravest souls would be hesitant to admit such a thing in front of all their church friends. But if you were suddenly struck blind, you would not hesitate to confess any sin if it meant getting your vision back. Immediately, he told me his story. A few years before, he had found magazines under his father's bed and became addicted to pornography. His voice broke and tears rolled down his face as I led him through a prayer of asking God to forgive him and renouncing his involvement in pornography. As the last word left his mouth, his eyesight returned. He received Jesus into His life in a most humble and beautiful way and his entire countenance changed as the peace of God came to replace the fear and torment he had experienced minutes earlier.

As Lois ministered to this young man, the rest of the kids cried, shook, laughed, and held onto each other. At one point, several of the young girls sang loudly and worshipped God. We kept moving along, ministering and imparting the love of the Father to them.

As we did, many of the other leaders in the room, the same people who had so eagerly told us they were on board beforehand, became noticeably unhappy. Some forcibly grabbed as many kids as they could and took them outside into the night. It didn't work – as fast as they took them out, their friends ran outside and brought them back into the meeting. It was amazing that just a couple of hours earlier these same leaders had assured us they had seen all of this before. Now they were the proverbial deer caught in headlights.

Turning around, I (Rex) came face to face with the dark-haired boy who was the leader of the rowdy element of the youth and who we had seen making out during most of the message. Now, he stood before me, with tears in his eyes, and asked if I would pray for him. I put my hand on his shoulder and asked God to come and touch him with His love. I could not think of anything else to say so I just stood and watched as the Holy Spirit moved upon him, and he wept. I looked over his shoulder and saw the speaker and the camp manager outside the main door. As they spoke, they became more animated, pointing in my direction. I got the feeling they were not in favor of what was happening.

Even from a distance, I could tell that whatever was being said was not casting us in a good light. Things were going to come to a head and soon. Within seconds, the speaker was back in the room and standing at my side. "Does he need to fall down too?" he asked me. I kept my hand on the boy's shoulder and said, "No, he does not 'need' to fall down."

I tried to steer the speaker to a more private area of the room, but he wasn't moving. "Do you know his name?" he asked me. I didn't; I hadn't even thought to ask him. "No," I said. "Do you know if he is saved?" he asked. I shook my head, "No."

"You don't even know if he is saved and you are asking him to be filled with the Holy Spirit," the speaker said. Before I could point out that I wasn't asking the Holy Spirit to fill him, but just asking God to come and minister to him, the speaker spoke again. "Don't you know about the four spiritual laws?"

I didn't know what to say, so I gently led the young man to a bench where we could sit. "Why don't we ask him what is happening to him. He is hearing everything we are saying," I said to the speaker. Settled on the bench, I asked the young man one simple question: "What is going on with you?"

He opened his tear-filled eyes, and in a broken voice said, "I didn't know, I didn't know how much I hurt Him and I am so sorry, I am so sorry. I asked Him to forgive me for the things I have done, I didn't know how much it hurt Him. I asked Him to come into my heart also and I know He has." As he spoke, I counted off all four spiritual laws the speaker had just said needed to happen. He knew he was a sinner and that God loved him. He knew the wages of sin was death. He repented of his sins. He asked Jesus for forgiveness for his sins. And he asked Jesus into his life.

God does not need our words to explain everything. He uses us as His vessels when we come along to be partakers in His glory. The speaker was speechless, but it did not last for very long as he looked at the young man and said, "I know Rex will not be here tomorrow, but if you would like to know more about God and to be filled with the Holy Spirit you can see me tomorrow and I will pray for you." The young man lifted his head and looked at the speaker. With the smoldering eyes of someone who had been hurt by authority over and over, he said, "I don't think I would ever come to you." He got up and left. Many times, I wondered what happened to that young man who God touched that night in 1995. I still find myself praying for him 20 years later, asking that God would keep him safe and draw him to Himself.

As ministry time closed, we spent another hour talking with the speaker about the revival. He was a pastor's son and said he had seen many a revival, and he assured us this was "not what a revival looked like." With a patience that comes only with a heavy anointing of the Holy Spirit, we listened and answered his harsh words with soft replies until we knew we could do no more.

Despite the criticism, we were glad and honored to have been used by God that night. We watched Him demonstrate His amazing, unfathomable love and power on His beloved kids in that most beautiful of places. May He be given all glory, and honor, for His unchanging love and unquenchable fire.

WHEN THE FIRE FALLS

Chapter 6

THE EARLY YEARS

Our church background no doubt framed our perception of what was happening. Raised in a Free Methodist church, Lois had a soft heart for God and gave her heart to Jesus at an early age. Her family went through some traumatic events including the divorce of her parents, which, combined with the hippie era, strongly influenced her to rebel against God in her teen years. After we were married and had moved to Montana, Lois rededicated her life to the Lord – almost a year before Rex gave his heart to Jesus in 1980. Before that, Rex had never gone to church and had no concept of what was acceptable church etiquette. Everything was new to him: ushers, programs, hymns, pews, stained glass windows, offerings, and visitors' cards.

We attended the church where Rex had accepted Jesus, part of a Church of God denomination headquartered in Anderson, Indiana. Later we would find that it was important to let people know where their headquarters were because there was another denomination that called itself 'Church of God,' based out of Cleveland, Tennessee. One was very Evangelical, and the other was very Pentecostal.

Our church put a strong emphasis on holiness, evangelism and sound Biblical doctrine, which we are thankful for as it gave us a solid foundation for our Christian walk. However, other than its strong emphasis on evangelism, it did not have a favorable view of the other gifts of the Spirit. As an adult Sunday school teacher, Rex himself taught that the gift of tongues was not for today. He was very persuasive in his presentation, Lois recalls. We weren't opposed to the moving of the Holy Spirit, but we had been told by church leaders that some other Christians emphasized things that were on the peripheral of the Scriptures and became out of balance in their theology (they called those people "Pentecostals"). In fact, our church had gone through two major splits before we arrived. Both resulted in church plants in our small town – one an Assembly of God, the other a Full Gospel. God had come and moved powerfully in our church but, because the manifestation of tongues had broken out, there was a church split. Needless to say, the church we spent our first ten years in took a dim view of both the gift of tongues and the gift of prophecy.

I (Rex) was thirty years old when I came to know Jesus as my Savior and knew nothing about the Bible or church culture. I read the Bible from cover to cover within the first six months of my conversion and was excited about the stories of Jesus and His disciples. From the beginning, I desired to do the very things they did in the Bible but was informed that those things do not happen in the church anymore. It was the first time I had ever heard the word, "dispensationalist." I didn't like it but, not knowing anything different, I accepted it.

Almost a year later, an older man in the church gave me a book on revival. It recounted what happened in the Azusa Street Revival meetings in Los Angeles in the early twentieth century. After reading it, I got pretty excited and showed it to one of the men who had led me to the Lord – the same man who told me that we "just don't do those things anymore."

"God used the gifts of the Spirit to establish the church in the beginning and sometimes He will allow the gifts to be used to establish new works," he told me. This got me even more excited; there must have been a call on my life to start a new work because I wanted to see the miracles that the disciples and the people at Azusa Street had seen.

Shortly after, our pastor returned from a two-year sabbatical at the Dallas Theological Seminary. On his way back from Dallas, he visited the Vineyard Church in Anaheim, California. When he arrived back at our church in 1983, he brought with him new worship songs from the Vineyard, introducing us to their style of worship. There were times his body would begin to tremble uncontrollably, which he told us was the Holy Spirit on him. People he prayed for would also become emotionally overwhelmed, cry and even shake. I asked him once to pray for me. He held out his trembling hands toward me. I felt nothing. I wanted to, but there was nothing.

Another couple from the Anaheim Vineyard moved into the area and became friends with our pastor. One day he called and asked us to come meet them. We did and, after a while, they asked if they could pray for us. It was our first experience with this kind of personal prayer; we had only known corporate, full-church prayer. They invited us to their home and said they knew the Holy Spirit wanted them to minister to us. We both sat, with the man praying for Rex and his wife praying for Lois. Not much happened to Rex; no physical manifestations, no trembling, crying or much emotion.

Lois, on the other hand, had a different experience. I (Lois) remember a powerful wave of God coming over me and I shook and cried uncontrollably. I wasn't afraid. It was as if my heart was being so overwhelmed with His love and goodness that I couldn't contain the emotions within me. As the waves of His power and love kept flowing over me, I felt incredible remorse for the sins I had committed and I remembered the sorrow I had gone through in the traumatic events of my childhood. This couple asked me questions and they had me pray to forgive others, repent for my own sin, and asked the Holy Spirit to come in and heal my deep wounds. After a while, I had to get up and go to the bathroom, but I was afraid that this amazing and incredible power of God would leave me if I did. It is indescribable when He touches you in this way.

Before that powerful encounter with the Holy Spirit, I would have random thoughts whisper to me, "You were saved before and you could never make it, you are no good and you will just sin again, you might as well give up now." Since that day, those tormenting thoughts have never come back. God delivered me from demonic influences that had still had rights to torment me through the un-repented sin that had been left in a hidden corner of my heart. The Holy Spirit knows everything about us and He comes to set us free in all areas, healing every wound with His love. He has come in His manifest power at different times in my life since that day. These high mark experiences are what I call "baptisms of His love and a fresh filling of the Holy Spirit." When the faithful, loving Father captures your heart, it isn't difficult to follow and obey Him. The fruit of the Spirit is made manifest through His presence, alive in us, and there is none that can ever fill this place in our hearts but Him.

One night, the pastor, Rex and three other leaders from the church were in the office for their monthly meeting. The pastor talked about how he had been touched powerfully by the Holy Spirit in Anaheim. He said it was for everyone and each one of us could experience it as well. "If that's true, pray that we too would receive what you're experiencing," I (Rex) said. The five of us went to the sanctuary. When I turned around, our pastor was lying on the front pew trembling from head to foot. I must admit I was a little annoyed; after all, he was the one who was supposed to be praying for us. I asked him what he wanted us to do. He looked up at me and said, "Just start praying!"

I went to one of the men and asked the Holy Spirit to touch him like he had touched our pastor. Suddenly, he began to tremble and soon was shaking violently. Before long, he was sobbing uncontrollably. Being new to all of this and not knowing what to do, I asked him why he was crying. "I feel like there is a wall in front of me and I just can't get through the wall and Jesus is on the other side of the wall," he said. I did the only thing I could think of doing and said, "Lord, take down the wall so he can see You."

His shaking intensified and he seemed to radiate. His arms and hands flapped so much it was like someone was blowing a fan directly in my face. He beamed with the glory of God and he said, "The love, the love, His love is pouring over me." I was excited and turned back to my pastor, who had propped himself up on his elbow so he could see what was happening. "You're right! We all can pray and experience this," I said.

The pastor motioned me closer to him. "Rex, I can see you have a demon."

"What!" I said. "Really? How can we get rid of it?" He told me not to worry, and called his Vineyard friend to come help him. For close to two hours, they worked at casting the demon out of me. I want you to know that whatever it was that the pastor had seen I was more than willing to have it gone. I confessed every sin I had ever committed, thought of committing, or might possibly commit in the future. At one point, they thought they had the demon trapped in my leg, then it was in my arm, then they were trying to get it out through my hand. Finally, exhausted, I said, "Guys, it's one o'clock in the morning and I have to drive home and get up in five hours to go to work. I have confessed everything I know to confess and I want to go home."

I drove the nine miles through the mountains to our home, parked the car and walked the few hundred feet to the house in the black, moonless night. I had such a peace about me that it never occurred to me to be afraid. Unfortunately for Lois, the pastor had called her right after I left the church and said, "Your husband has a demon, we tried to get it out of him but couldn't. So your demon-possessed husband is on his way home." As you could imagine, she was not sure of who or what she was meeting at the door, but we talked, prayed and went to bed. Since that night, I've never been made aware again of any demon that needed to be cast out of me. This was my first look into the wacky world of those whose immature attempts to operate in the realm of the power of the Holy Spirit can drive a person away from anything supernatural.

The pastor continued to misunderstand how to lead us in the ways of the Holy Spirit, eventually going off the deep end and being asked to leave the church. But we had tasted God's presence and we were hungry for more. A trip to Tacoma, Washington, to a Vineyard meeting left us disappointed, so we went to hear

Vineyard founder John Wimber preach at a 1986 conference in Columbia, South Carolina. We sat in the very back row and every morning we held hands and prayed that God would protect us from anything not of Him. After John spoke, he asked the Holy Spirit to come; it was the most amazing thing to witness. You could physically see the reactions of the people as the Holy Spirit swept across the room. We will never forget watching the reaction of the people to the Holy Spirit and feeling the presence of God as He passed over us.

We left excited about the things of God and the working of the Holy Spirit. We devoured material on the gifts and started a home group that, even in those early days, became known for the presence and power of the Holy Spirit. We were blessed to meet John Wimber's son, who was in the area hunting with a friend of ours and stopped over to visit. However, as we moved into the late 1980s, our excitement for the things of God waned, and as our friend, Pastor Che Ahn of the Pasadena Vineyard has said: "It seemed like the late eighties were from Hades. It's like God just up and left."

In 1990, we moved to Kalispell, Montana, and attended a Christian Missionary Alliance church. Soon we were part of their leadership team. For the first few years, the church lived under the mantra, "We are a hospital for the soul." If you had been hurt by the church or by the circumstances of life, our church was a safe place to come. We would not hurry you into serving or ministering but would give you time to heal and enjoy just being a Christian. We did the best we could and I believe God answered the cry of our hearts. However, God was about to show us a much better plan and in 1995, God came in power, showering us with His love and mercy and showing us what His idea of being "a hospital for the soul" was.

A year before the outpouring, a stranger asked me (Rex) where I went to church. I told him and he said, "Oh! You are Baha'i Faith!"

"Why would you say that?" I asked.

"Because you have the Baha'i Faith symbols over your building," he answered.

"What symbols?" I said.

"Those two interlocking circles over the building, those represent the Baha'i faith religion," he said.

I was an elder and knew nothing about the meaning of the symbol. You could have knocked me over with a feather. Two nights later, we had an elders' meeting and I asked if they knew about this. "Oh yes!" they all said. "The architect of the building was Baha'i faith and he put those symbols on top of the building. We were hoping to reach him for Christ so we just let him do it." I couldn't believe it.

"I'm going to take those symbols down because people think we are a Baha'i faith church," I said. In classic church leadership fashion, they said the idea would have to go to the governing board to see if there was any money available to do the job.

"I have the money and I'll have a crane here this week to take those symbols down," I said. By the end of the week, the symbols were on their way to the dump.

A few months later, I felt pain in the little toe of my left foot. It was strange and, within days, the pain traveled up my left leg to the calf, turning into a numbing sensation. I went to a chiropractor who worked on me, but nothing changed. Two weeks went by and the numbness spread to the other leg and all the way up to my waist. By the time we could see a doctor, I was numb from the waist down. The doctor sent me to a neurologist, who ordered an MRI.

It was a sclerosis, the neurologist said, ordering a brain MRI and a spinal tap. It was only one, so it wasn't multiple sclerosis, but the numbness continued to increase until I had zero feeling around my waist and my legs had become so numb that I was almost in need of a cane.

During one of the procedures, our pastor and an elder came in and prayed. I (Lois) felt that God had answered their prayers. I also prayed to cancel any demonic spirits that would have any right to attack my husband. However, since we were not sure that Rex was healed, he continued to take the medicine the doctors prescribed and follow their instructions until we could see a change.

Praise God, our prayers were answered and the symptoms disappeared, except for the occasional twinge in Rex's little toe on his left foot. We were so blessed to have Rex healed, it was confirmation to us that the hand of God was on him. Looking back, we believe the physical attack on Rex and our family was in direct relationship to removing the occult symbols over the church. The enemy wanted to take him out before the coming outpouring of the

Holy Spirit on our family.

When you take the time to look back over your life, you can see the hand of God leading you to a place of destiny and purpose. From the beginning of our story, God's hand has been upon us. If at any time we had allowed the enemy the opportunity to discourage us enough to give up, it's possible none of what we are writing about would have happened.

There are no easy choices, no easy paths to travel. The cross that we carry has been made especially for us, but with God's help and the Holy Spirit's guidance, we will finish the race set before us. The enemy is real and he will do anything to stop us from doing what God has called us to do. As we look back over our lives, we are amazed at the victories that have come because we persevered through mountains of adversity. It is an honor to say yes to God and to recognize that His ways are far above our own plans. Be faithful, ask for the power to be victorious, and believe in the One who walks with you.

The enemy tried to destroy us but failed, thanks to the grace of God and the power of His name. A few months after Rex was healed, we were at church when our worship pastor came running down the stairs and gave us a pamphlet to a conference in Kelowna, British Columbia. Saying yes to God changed our family's lives forever. We give Him all glory and honor as we press on toward the mark to win the prize He has set before us.

Chapter 7

JESUS PLACE

The phone rang. It was late – after 11 – and our daughter Krista was frantic on the other end of the line. Both our girls were driving home with four friends from a young adult meeting in Whitefish, Montana. We listened as Krista anxiously tried to explain something about a mysterious "man in black" that had appeared at the meeting, walking, almost gliding, around the young people as they lay on the floor. Now Krista said the spirit man in black was in their car –and from what we could hear of the other kids in the background, we knew they thought so too.

Hoping to calm her down, we asked that she start from the beginning and tell us what happened. Krista said that God had moved powerfully at the meeting and she had found herself lying on the floor with many other kids. At one point, she felt something go by her and she opened her eyes and saw a man, dressed all in black, including a black cape, walking amongst the kids on the floor. Krista looked over at one of her friends who had opened her eyes as well and they both watched the man in black as he walked by. Then he just disappeared.

They thought this very weird, and in the car on the way home, the others were very skeptical of their story. Just as Krista told them how the man in black had disappeared in the meeting, they all suddenly saw him standing at the edge of the road. They screamed, and then he appeared in the back of the car with them.

That's when Krista called us. In the background, we could hear the other kids freaking out. We asked her where they were and from what she told us, we knew that in ten minutes they would be home.

We hung up the phone and got ready. We got out some anointing oil and talked about what we needed to do. As it was a warm night, we heard them drive into the property, and before the car had stopped, we could hear the kids (both male and female) as they got out of the car. They were distraught. These were tough young adults – kids I had never seen cry or become upset by any circumstance. However, as they walked up to the house, you could tell they were beside themselves. Even the older boys cried and shook. As they came into the house, we anointed each of them with oil and prayed for them, commanding any unclean or demonic spirits to leave in the name of Jesus and in His power and authority.

Soon they were inside and all talking at once about what they had experienced. Even though it was only Krista and her friend who had seen the man walking around the floor, the others all saw the same person they had described standing on the side of the road, and they were all convinced that he had materialized in the back of their car. Given their concern, we weren't going to dispute it.

As they spoke, our beagle began to stink. This was more than just a skunk smell; it was a horrific foul odor. We picked the dog up, put her outside in her small cage, and came back inside to be with the kids. We walked around the house praying, anointing with oil and commanding any foul spirit to leave in the name of Jesus. Then we went back outside, anointed our dog with oil and commanded the demonic spirit to leave her in the name of Jesus too. The odor immediately left her. We brought her back inside and she was perfectly fine without a trace of the odor she had smelled of before we had prayed.

A few days later in one of our church elder meetings, I started to tell them what had happened to our kids. One of the elders held up his hand and stopped me. He told us about the man in black. He said that for years, a demonic spirit looking like a man in black with a cape had appeared to the Native Americans on the reservation and had created quite a stir with each appearance. Krista and her friends' description of him was exactly what the elder said he had heard described for years from those east of the Rockies and up into Canada. He said he had seen the man in black himself and it raised the hair on his neck.

The meeting that the kids attended that night was a weekly Sunday night gathering called the Jesus Place. A young and anointed worship leader from New Jersey had moved into the area and started leading worship in a local mall. Two brothers who were being used of God happened to see him there and started attending. The brothers were instrumental in bringing the kids to the meeting and before long they attracted 200 young people from various churches and off the streets. They danced and worshipped and sang for hours and hours, and there was a lot of spontaneous song and the prophetic. Before the man in black, our kids had asked us to stay away – after all, who wants to be seen with their parents, even as cool as *we* are? However, after what happened, they asked that we come to the next meeting.

The next Sunday, I (Rex) went to the meeting. I stuck out like a sore thumb – in the entire room, there were only ten adults among all the kids. The leader told everyone to get in groups and pray for each other. Not knowing anyone other than our kids and some of their friends, I went over to a group of adults and asked if I could join them. "No!" snapped one of the men, but three of them moved past him and stood in front of me, asking if I would pray for them. I didn't recognize any of them, but I thought perhaps they had come to a Thursday night meeting at our church and knew me from there. I prayed and all the adults were soon on the floor – except the man who had said no; he went and sat against the wall. From there I just kept praying and more and more people were overwhelmed by God. The floor was soon full.

There were so many unsaved kids coming to the gathering that it was an evangelist's dream. The music drew the crowds and it was definitely the 'in' place to be on a Sunday night. It was also a safe place to be, and the worship leader kept things going very well.

On one Sunday evening, as there was a moment of silence in the worship, we heard the strange sound of a flute in the background. Looking around, I (Lois) saw a young, long-haired man playing continuously on a long wooden flute. As I made my way over to him, I could smell an unclean spirit. Without the young man hearing me, I found myself canceling its assignment and commanding the spirit to leave in the name of Jesus. He quickly found his way out of the building.

We continued to come back on Sunday nights and became part of the leadership team. It was a very powerful time, and we were honored and blessed to be a part of it. We prayed for most of these kids many times and some were touched so powerfully that they eventually went to the mission field or into full-time ministry. Being around them was an adventure and always exciting.

After a summer and fall of meeting in parks around the Flathead Valley, the weather turned chilly. We desperately searched for a place indoors to meet the following Sunday. We asked all the kids present, fifty of them, to get in a circle under one of the park pavilions to pray that we would find a place to meet inside again.

Most of the kids prayed that God would lead us to the right place. One of them, who didn't always quote Scripture as precisely as possible, took his turn. With a humble heart, he prayed for our worship leader, asking God to give him some new songs. I (Rex) was standing next to a close pastor friend of mine and we exchanged a knowing look – the young man had prayed what most of us were thinking, but never had the nerve to say. His next prayer, however, cracked us up. "Lord," he prayed as he tried to correctly remember Ephesians 6:16, "help him to extinguish the fiery farts of the enemy." My friend and I hit the floor howling; the correct reference is "Extinguish the fiery darts of the wicked" – but this worked too.

Another time, friends of ours brought a group of freshly saved kids down from British Columbia. At the time, we had helped plant a church called The Father's House, where we met. One of the elders greeted the kids telling them how glad we were they came, and how much we loved them. One young man, with a big metal stud pierced through the middle of his tongue, headed over to the elder, hugged him, and did an enormous lick up the side of his face. We were shocked. He licked the entire side of the elder's face!

The elder was livid and told everyone the meetings were over. Of course, he didn't have the authority to stop them, but he never came back after that. My feeling was that this kid, who was homeless and just saved, had heard people say that they loved him and then later abuse, molest and abandon him. I wondered if he was thinking, "Why not just cut to the chase and see if the love this guy was spouting was real and would last or just be good until the first time I screwed up?"

After the lick, the meetings were powerful. I (Rex) spoke at one of the sessions that day, and as I talked about the "latter rain," a torrential rain came in. Talk about a divine coincidence! The rain came down so hard that no one could hear what I was saying so they all went outside. A couple of the guys came back inside, drenched to the bone, and ran toward me. I gave them the biggest bear hugs they had ever received. It was like hugging a soaked sponge; at the end, I was as drenched as they were.

The young worship leader God had sent to the valley was incredible. He just worshipped straight from his heart, a heart that was after God's heart for the lost. We worshipped and danced with the kids for hours and we prayed for the Holy Spirit to come and change us from the inside out. It was common to see kids off the street touched by God's power and love, shake and sob, and give their hearts to Jesus. Many young girls were touched and I (Lois) loved being there to minister to them as a mother, representing His unconditional love and acceptance. I was as transformed by these experiences as they were. Our own daughter Tonya was water baptized in Whitefish Lake on a beautiful Montana summer night.

We were so proud of her and excited to see her baptized with her friends and reconfirm her dedication to follow God. What amazing memories we have of those days.

Most things last only for a season and the Jesus Place was like that. Sweeping over the valley, it was a safe place where God touched the lives of many kids, much like the Jesus movement of the 1960s. Sometimes we measure success by things like longevity, but God measures success by the hearts transformed by His love. One day, we will see the full measure of those touched by God and how their lives were affected for eternity.

WHEN THE FIRE FALLS

Chapter 8

THE JOURNEY CONTINUES

We first met Randy Clark within a few years of the outpouring that began for us in 1995. Our friendship with the Clarks has been a very important part of our journey. After Kelowna, which was birthed by the outpouring in Toronto that Randy was instrumental in starting, we just kept pursuing God. We were used as fire starters to bring a fresh outpouring of the Holy Spirit into our community and church. Because of this, we both felt a responsibility to those who had experienced this touch from God. This led us to continually go and listen, observe others affected by this move of God, and to study historical revivals. More importantly, we searched the Scriptures to make sure we were following God and staying true to His Word. We discovered the more of His love and power we received, the more we had to give away. We were in constant need of His refreshing.

A year after the outpouring started, one of the former elders of Jack Deere's Presbyterian church asked us to assist in a new church plant in Whitefish, Montana. Since Jack traveled as an itinerant speaker, he kept in close contact with the fledgling church. He suggested the four leaders in charge of the plant go to Kansas City to a conference where the main leaders of the revival were gathering. It was a who's who of the charismatic zoo, as everyone associated with the renewal was there.

It was at that meeting in 1997 that I (Rex) saw Randy Clark for the first time. I sat behind him and his friend Lance Wallnau at a morning session. After a break, I came back to my chair and saw, right in front of me, Randy's Bible sitting on his chair. For a brief second, I wondered if Randy's Bible had any special anointing on it and if God would still honor that anointing if I took it. I had to laugh to myself because I just could not see how God would bless a stolen Bible, much less bless the person that took it. I did not realize it then but in just a few short years, one of my principal jobs would be to ensure that Randy's Bible would not be lost or stolen. God's sense of humor is not lost on me!

One of the prophets at the meeting stood up to speak. The prophet was in rare form that night in Kansas City. On one occasion, he pointed to a woman, had her stand up and prophesied that her name was Amanda Grace (I can't remember the correct name, but this is close). The woman said that wasn't her name. He repeated the name again and said he was sure she was the right person. The woman again said that was not her name. Shaking his head, he repeated the name. The woman said Grace was indeed her last name, but Amanda was not her first name. Confused, he asked if she was sure.

"Amanda used to be my first name, but not anymore," she said. "I took on a different first name and Amanda is now my middle name."

"Well, you may have changed your first name, but God knows you as Amanda Grace," the prophet said. I was amazed by the exhibition of the prophetic gift.

Next, he called a young man up and not only told him his

full name but also his age. The young man grinned and told him he was not that old. The prophet asked him if he was sure and the young man said his birthday was not until tomorrow and he was sure of it. At that point, his dad stood up, put his hand on his son's shoulder, and said, "Son, we're from Florida and there is a one hour time difference from Florida to Kansas City. It's 11:05 P.M. here, which makes it tomorrow in Florida. Son, this is your birthday."

He called the four of us from Montana to stand up, which we were happy to do. We were all wondering what the prophet was going to say about us. We stood and assumed the position, standing with our hands out and eyes closed. For more than half an hour, we stood there, as the prophet ignored us and went off on one of his stories. After a while, I wondered if he even remembered us standing there but finally he came back to us. The first part of the prophecy was for the other three men but I and others felt the last piece was for me in particular. He said, "You will be chasing out more demons than you could ever imagine, all the way from the Father's House to the Capitol!" We had just named the church we planted in Montana, The Father's House, so we could see how that was significant. We felt the last part, "All the way to the Capitol," had to do with the Capitol in Washington, D.C. However, we lived in Montana and had no wish to live anywhere else. We didn't know it then, but within five years, we moved to live just a little more than two hours north of Washington.

After the prophetic word, we went from being nobodies to instant celebrities. I find it amazing how a prophecy can change someone's impression of you. Those pastors who previously ignored us were now coming up and giving us their business cards.

Randy came and told me that he was about to do a conference in Florence, Kentucky, with pastors from Argentina. The Argentineans would share on the revival that was taking place in their South American nation, and teach on how they set people free in their deliverance tents. Randy felt that if the word was right, it would be good for us to attend. We all made plans to go and, within a month, we found ourselves at the conference. It was a wild, significant time for Lois and me.

We heard tremendous teaching on the revival in Argentina, along with how to set people free using the ten step model of deliverance that Carlos Annacondia uses in his crusades. Pablo Bottari, the man who organized the tents for Carlos and who developed the model through his experiences in ministering to newly saved converts, taught. This is still the method that Lois and I use and it is highly effective in bringing freedom to the broken ones and to the captives, doing it all in the power and authority of Jesus Christ. This method is done with His love and with dignity shown to the person. It doesn't concentrate on demons, but on the person God loves who needs freedom and healing.

As the conference progressed, we found ourselves sitting next to a peculiar (in a good way) couple. No matter where we seemed to sit, they always ended up sitting right next to us. We got along with them right away, it just seemed like we clicked. They eventually told us they worked for Randy and traveled around the world with him. They told us they felt this was not a chance meeting and asked us to keep in touch because they sensed from God that something was going to come out of our meeting.

We stayed connected and they told us about a trip Randy was planning to Argentina and Brazil, and wondered if we would like to go along. We signed up right away for the 21-day mission. Unfortunately, the trip was cancelled because of severe flooding in the part of Argentina we planned to visit.

I met Randy again in Toronto a couple of months later. I thanked him for the opportunity to accompany him on the trip. It was evident he didn't know me from Adam, or that we were going to be part of the group going with him to Argentina. He did say that the trip had just been rescheduled, and that all the same people were going to be called to see if they wanted to still go. When I got back to my seat, I told Lois what Randy had said and we were both very excited for what God was divinely putting together.

Randy spoke at one of the Toronto sessions and at the end of his talk, he said he did not have time to pray for people individually but he would say a general prayer over those who came forward. I felt the word was for me, so about twenty people, including myself, went up. As we stood there, Randy looked at us and said, "Only twenty! I guess I will have time to pray for you individually." Between the time he turned to place his Bible on the pulpit and came down the steps to where we were standing, more than 100 people rushed to the front to get in on personal ministry from Randy. I now found myself at the end of a very long line of people but it was worth it – even as I waited, I received a wonderful vision from God. Just as the vision ended, Randy touched my forehead and I fell to the floor.

In a strange turn of events, the couple we had met in Kentucky quit working for Randy just before the rescheduled trip. Of the dozen people who went to South America, we were the only people Randy did not know or even remember meeting. For us, it was our first real international trip outside North America. We were nervous and excited.

We went to Argentina first, where we visited the Vision of the Future churches of Pastor Omar Caberra. When we got there, we learned Omar's wife was quite sick so we never got to meet him, but we did travel with his son, Omar Caberra Jr., which was a treat in itself. Omar was very hospitable and took excellent care of us all.

Omar told some amazing stories of events he had witnessed while growing up and traveling with his father. Omar Sr. had birthed the Vision of the Future churches on signs and wonders. Once, he went to Santa Maria and visited the small church he had planted there. While there, he prayed for a young boy who was born without any ears; the child had only holes on the side of his head where his ears should have been. Even with the holes, he couldn't hear. Omar said his father put both hands over the places where his ears should have been and prayed. A small bubble appeared on each side of the boy's head and as the bubbles grew, they formed the most perfect ears. The boy heard clearly for the first time. The little church of 75 people was greatly blessed. Omar went on his way but within a couple of days the pastor from Santa Maria called asking for help. Once word got out around town about what had happened to the little boy, the church had grown to more than 10,000 people. Vision of the Future churches had become the fastest growing churches in Argentina and we could see why.

We got the chance to go to Santa Maria and it was quite interesting. During ministry time, God seemed to move in pockets. Each of us on the prayer team had small pockets of people around us and the anointing to heal in Jesus' name was powerful. But if you stepped out of your circle of anointing, it seemed like nothing happened. We quickly learned to stay in our pockets. A big, black Labrador dog wandered into the meeting late that night. It was well after midnight and we were all tired. As he walked by us, Lois and I laid our hands on his head and said, "More, Lord." The dog staggered over to another couple and they reached down and did the same thing; the dog collapsed to the floor. The dog laid there, unmoving, for two hours with people stepping over him the entire time.

After an incredible week traveling and visiting the Vision of the Future churches in Argentina, we went on to Sao Paulo, Brazil. Sao Paulo is a grand city of more than twenty million people. The first night we stayed in a hotel and had the opportunity to take an elevator up to the top floor and, looking around, all we could see were tall skyscrapers. There were more lights around us in that hotel than we had seen in a lifetime. What an amazing sight!

Our journey with God just kept increasing. It grew because we were simply pursuing God and saying yes to Him every time He orchestrated and confirmed within us the next step to take. He is an amazing God and we are, and will always be, grateful to have been chosen to be His ambassadors to bring His fire and unfathomable love. He brings salvation, freedom and healing to a broken world.

WHEN THE FIRE FALLS

Chapter 9

CREATION COMES ALIVE

I (Rex) buried my hands in my face to keep thousands of mosquitos from devouring me as I knelt in the South American jungle, high up on the side of a mountain. One of the men who led us up the mountain trail gave us newspapers to cover the ground and keep our pants from being soaked by the damp earth. Torrential rains ended just as we arrived. It was after 3 a.m. and we were tired.

Beside me, Lois gasped. "Rex, open your eyes and look around you! The twigs and leaves are glowing!" I opened my eyes to a sight I will never forget. The jungle floor where I was praying had begun to light up. Within seconds, those around us had also started to notice that the twigs and leaves were glowing in the pitch-black surroundings. It was as if creation came alive right before our eyes. Mesmerized, we picked up the little twigs and leaves, marveling at the florescent light that was emanating from within them. After a while, our hands glowed in the pitch-black, cloudy night from the twigs and leaves they held.

It was March 1999 and our first time in Brazil. We had finished in Argentina with Omar Cabrera Jr., and arrived late into Sao Paulo the night before. After spending our first night in a hotel, the twelve of us on the trip had been separated, each couple going to a different private home to sleep. Early that morning, the van picked us up for the first of three meetings scheduled for the day.

As I settled into my seat, one of the men on our team leaned forward and, far too excited for the time of day it was, told us, "Guys, you are not going to believe what I heard last night! Pastor Dierco told me they have a mountain that once a month they go to and pray on for the entire Saturday night." Seeing we were not impressed, he continued, "All week prior to this they have a water fast and on Saturday evening they climb this mountain and come down Sunday morning after being up all night praying and worshipping. Then they go to their church for communion."

As a team, we were exhausted, although humbled by the church's commitment. Our friend Steve wasn't done. "There's more. When they're up on this mountain they find a spot that no human has been on. They hack their way through the jungle with machetes until they find a spot and then they begin to pray and sing. As they continue, it's not uncommon for them to start to see things happening around them. The jungle comes alive with light as the leaves and twigs start to glow. They have seen tree trunks at least ten foot up glow as if they were florescent lights. What appears as tiny fireflies at a distance become bigger and bigger till they are close to 18 inches in diameter then burst into rainbows of color and light."

Steve had our attention now. We were riveted, mouths hanging open. "And do you want to hear something else?" he asked. We all nodded. "They're going up there tomorrow night and they want to know if we're interested in going along with them."

We couldn't say yes fast enough.

The next night, the bus pulled out at close to two in the morning. We were exhausted and, to be honest, our spirits and bodies were half wanting to go to the mountain and half longing to go to bed. Knowing we would be up all night and facing meetings scheduled for the next day fed our tiredness. Yet weaving through the city, I (Lois) felt the presence of God on that bus and it transformed what I saw in the streets of Brazil while most of the others were asleep. There was a withered man with no legs crawling with his arms to get to some garbage in the gutter. On the next block, I saw, for the first time in my life, a transvestite. He was a very tall man in a red dress, with full facial makeup, lipstick, high heels and shaved legs, walking along the side of the street. I wept for them both and felt God's heart for the ones He came to save.

In a city of twenty million people, there is always action. The streets were alive with people but the further we got from the city, the less activity we saw. Our bus stopped and we stumbled out into the night. We were an odd bunch of people; two of our group were in their late 70s, all of the women wore dresses, and a few of them had sandals on their feet. Not exactly "let's go jungle hiking" apparel. Our guides pointed to the trail before us and off we went up the mountain. The path was steep and slippery from the torrential rains, and we had to help each other up the windy trail as it became extremely difficult without each other's assistance. Every now and then we could hear others in the distance and eventually we made out the sounds of people worshipping. From the sounds we heard, there must have been several groups up on the mountain in different locations that night.

After a while, the machetes came out as the men began to hack a path into the jungle and then cleared a spot that was big enough for all of us. One of the men with us had brought a guitar and was singing worship songs, so we joined in as we each found a place to kneel on the wet ground. As I (Rex) knelt, I wondered what to pray for. I found out later that I was not the only one wrestling with those kinds of thoughts that night; I think all of us struggled.

"This is stupid," I said to myself. "I just want God and I don't care if anything lights up." I drifted off and on in prayer, almost falling asleep at times and then pulling myself back to pray. I cried out to God. "All I want is You! Nothing else matters, just You!" I even thanked God that we took the time to get our shots for typhoid fever before we left. With thousands of mosquitoes buzzing around me I couldn't help but think how wise that decision had been. That's when Lois tapped me on the shoulder and I noticed the soft glow starting around me.

Reaching out and picking up the glowing twigs and small leaves around me, it did not take long till my hands were filled with glowing vegetation. I showed one of the men and suddenly he reached out and took all the twigs and leaves that were in my hand and walked away. I wanted to say, "Hey! Why don't you get your own?" But as quickly as the thought came, it left; I picked some more off the jungle floor and soon my hands were overflowing once again.

What did it mean? This is always where we get into trouble. Having a western mindset that firmly believes in cause and effect, I have a built-in system that tries to logically figure everything out. I have entertained the thought that there was some kind of biological or nuclear dumping ground in the area or that I was just so tired that I saw what I wanted to see. The truth is that rational people try to use human reasoning to explain what we do not understand. That is why we have so much difficulty when we try to describe the indescribable. Is it any wonder that creation would come alive when we worship the Creator? Maybe we just don't recognize it because we have no paradigm for supernatural events. Perhaps instead of lowering our theology to the level of our experience, we should raise our experience to the level of our theology.

Whatever happened that night, it never made me want to worship piles of twigs and leaves. However, I did notice that when we stopped pressing into God in prayer and worship, and changed our focus into picking up the twigs and sticks, the level of what we experienced plateaued. I wonder what would have happened if we would have continued to focus in on Jesus. Would we have seen the tree trunks light up as others had been able to see? I would like to think so. I hope we can all learn to continue to press into God without being sidetracked by the manifestations that appear as we draw close to Him. A few days later, we were outside of Belo Horizonte and a group of us went out again late at night to the side of a mountain, but nothing happened.

We brought a bag of leaves and twigs back with us, and we still have them. We kept them in a bowl on our bedroom dresser for several months after our return from Brazil. One night after we had been out, our oldest daughter Krista asked us what those leaves and twigs were in our room. We had forgotten to tell her everything that had happened to us in Brazil.

We told her they were from Brazil and asked her why she

was interested in them. Krista said she had put some praise music on and was going about doing things and found herself walking back and forth from her bedroom to the bathroom, which had her passing in front of our open bedroom door. As she was singing along to the praise music, she noticed there was something glowing on our dresser. She came in and discovered the twigs and leaves were glowing; she was quite amazed as she looked at them.

Why should we be surprised that leaves would glow, or that rocks would cry out, in worship to our Creator and Lord?

Chapter 10

THE NIGHT THE LIGHTS WENT OUT

Randy and our team were hosted in Sao Paulo by the 1,200 foursquare churches in that city. The denomination was so large in Brazil that it had its own television and radio stations. The conference was called "Catch the Fire," and all of the pastors and their spouses were encouraged to attend. They took advantage of the denomination's resources by having both radio and TV coverage, which ran for all of the meetings.

As Randy spoke, the place overflowed with people. Brazil doesn't have the same kind of fire codes that are enforced in the United States, so you can crowd in as tightly as you want. It was a familiar sight to see the aisles packed with people, making it almost impossible to move up and down them. The balcony was also brimming with people and even the entryways were crammed full.

The meetings were only for pastors and their spouses, and the thick heavy cords for the TV crews were everywhere as men with big cameras on their shoulders tried to get shots from all angles. There was no air conditioning – it was uncomfortably hot, even though they put huge fans up on the platform to blow over the congregation. A place where the fans would blow on you became prime real estate.

The night progressed beautifully and God healed many of the people. Randy spoke a message we had already heard twice on the trip. But that night, he strayed from his usual pattern; he talked about sexual sin. He implored these church leaders to confess and turn away from their sin because that sin was holding the people in their congregations in bondage. We had become accustomed to Randy veering off subject as the Holy Spirit led him, so we weren't alarmed. What happened next, however, was amazing.

A wave of conviction from the Holy Spirit swept into the room and within minutes, the entire place was filled with cries and wails. Men and women, pastors and their spouses jumped from their seats and fought to get to the front. They fell to their knees in any available space, repented loudly as tears streaked down their faces. It was an intense surge of the presence and power of God that had come into the room.

At the start, those who repented did so very quietly. But as Randy continued to speak, the people lost their timidity and cried out to God to cleanse them from their sexual addictions. They were very loud and very specific. As the spirit of holiness became more pronounced the wails of the people that wanted to be set free reached a fever pitch.

As we stood along the platform, we watched the camera crews snap into action getting close-ups of the faces of the pastors, recording all that was happening. Lois and I looked at each other and realized that the cameras were filming the most intimate sins of these people and broadcasting them into the homes of literally millions for all to see and hear. Both of us felt panic rising up inside of us as to what this could mean for some of these leaders once they returned home.

Without warning, the lights went out and a thick blackness came over everything. There were no windows and it was pitch black. Randy's voice, now unamplified, could barely be heard over the loud roar of those coming to the front with their cries of repentance and anguish.

Within a short time, a man came from the back with a lit candle that sent dancing, flickering shadows around the crowded room. Randy continued to preach and somehow his voice rose above the roar and could be heard plainly. Oddly, it did not seem like anyone was aware that the lights had gone off, for no one stopped or even hesitated in their coming to the front to confess their sin and repent. The only ones who stopped were the camera crew that had just lost their power supply and were confused over what to do next. That lone candle illuminated the entire church enough that everyone could see to move around.

For more than three hours, the meeting room was bedlam, with tears and heartfelt repentance followed by laughter, restoration, and joy. Couples cried out and prayed through their sins, grabbed on to each other, and asked for forgiveness. Our team moved through, climbed over, and somehow made our way through the crowd, praying for as many as we could reach. The tiny candle stayed lit the entire time, giving everyone enough light to see.

The Holy Spirit began to lift off the meeting and we knew it was coming to an end. After the team regrouped at the front, the authorities told us the power outage was quite extensive and people were having trouble getting home due to traffic jams throughout the city. As we left, we talked about the strange events of the evening; the moment we stepped across the threshold of the church, all the lights came back on. We stood out on the sidewalk, amazed at the turn of events, knowing we had been a part of a supernatural occurrence.

The next morning, we learned that the strange blackout had spread to over a third of the city, affecting close to seven million people. The amazing thing is that as the city's electrical engineers tried to find out what caused the massive power outage, they had traced it back to the very block where we were having our meetings. They told us that it seemed a power surge had started from there and caused breakers to trip, affecting one substation after another, causing a chain reaction, and producing the massive power outage.

They could not figure out where the surge came from, but we had all witnessed and seen for ourselves the massive power surge of supernatural conviction that had swept through the building. There was no doubt in any of us that this was orchestrated by our merciful and all-powerful God. Whenever we remember the night the lights went out in Sao Paulo, we marvel again at His kindness and the supernatural protection He gave His beloved people.

Chapter 11

TAKING IT TO THE STREETS

Early in the revival, the Spirit of the Lord would come upon us and we would have visions and dreams. These events were very special to us, and although we did not always understand fully what they meant, we knew they were from God. The details we remembered after we awoke were so precise that we knew these were not ordinary dreams.

In one vision, I (Rex) saw myself flying over a major east coast city in a news helicopter, overlooking a major revival breaking out in the most desperate part of the inner city. It was a revival of the homeless; the abandoned building where they met glowed in the night air with the glory of God.

We had no reason to doubt the vision but we never planned to visit or live on the east coast. However, a few years later, we found ourselves living in Pennsylvania, only two hours from Baltimore, ninety minutes from Philadelphia, and three hours from Pittsburgh and New York City. It happened so fast it was like we woke up one morning and found ourselves living in the heart of several east coast cities. We remembered the vision, but had no idea how it could ever come to pass. Having a vision is one thing, but putting legs to it is another altogether.

After living in Pennsylvania for a couple of years, I would periodically get a phone call from a man who obviously had watched too many Rocky Balboa movies. "Hey, why don't youse come down to Philly and minister on the streets with me?" he'd ask in a thick East Philly accent, just like Rocky. He was persistent and called me at least three times over six months. Each time I graciously declined.

One day, I reminisced about the vision and bemoaned the fact I didn't know how I was ever going to see it come into reality. In my frustration, I asked the Lord when He was going to send someone to show me the way. As quickly as I said it, I felt the voice of the Lord saying, "How many times do I have to have him call you?" I knew immediately what He meant and within 24 hours, the man called again and asked me to go with him down to Philly. I said yes. Later, he told me that he wasn't going to call again but the Lord had told him the day before to give me one more chance.

That call was the beginning of five years of the most interesting friendship and ministry we have ever been part of. We had been born and raised in South Dakota, spent 21 years in Montana on small farms with a lot of space, and now, somehow, we found ourselves ministering in the worst area of Philadelphia, surrounded by drug addicts, prostitutes, and criminals. We were tossed into the deep end of a pool with no idea how to swim.

Over the next few months, we made several trips to Philly. Each time, we found it so far outside our comfort zone that we felt we were on another planet. The area we went was centered on Kensington Avenue, which is known throughout the city as the absolute worst place to go. We loaded up the back of our new friend's pickup with sandwiches, cakes, pie and coffee, found a street corner, and handed them out while talking to people about Jesus. The sweets were a big draw for heroin addicts and a sure way to get them over for prayer. It was not very safe – drug deals would happen right next to us and gang members would walk by with really big guns.

It was a major learning curve for us. Each place we went, and every person we talked to, seemed to be out of an old black and white 1950s movie. As doped up as many were, the people on the streets didn't often forget your name. Even though some of them could not remember their own name, because they had not used their real name in years, they always seemed to remember ours. Even the police thought we were crazy for being there and told us they did not want to get out of their cars – and they had on protective bulletproof vests!

After six months of sporadically going to Philly, our friend rented a 40 by 80 foot tent and put it up in Harrowgate Park, on the corner of Kensington and Tioga. Those three days and two nights in the heart of the hood was an experience nearly impossible to believe. We brought enough food to fill 200 bags with groceries. We had tables full of used clothing and school supplies to be handed out on Saturday morning. We grilled five hundred hamburgers and hot dogs with chips and sodas on Saturday and had testimonies and live worship music as much as possible, with CDs going the rest of the time.

You have not lived until you preach to a group of heroin addicts, pimps, prostitutes, and everything else in between. One thing we learned is to never ask a rhetorical question. Do not pose anything during one's talk that could easily be misconstrued as being a question that requires an immediate answer. This is tougher than it looks for preachers. If you say, "Have you ever felt like people don't understand you?" typically you will not get much of a response from a church congregation other than a nod of the head in agreement. That was not the case in Philly. That same vague question would get an immediate hand in the air and before you knew it, an out loud answer: "Yeah, yeah, pastor, I... I... get that a lot you know, it's like they..." and off they go until you are forced to interrupt them.

Some walked toward the speaker and just stood there, staring, trying to intimidate. Others were so infested with demons that they would periodically manifest while we were speaking. We learned we needed to make eye contact with them and tell them to "Stop, in the name of Jesus." Usually, they shook their heads and sat back down.

The City of Philadelphia had been trying to contain prostitution, newly released prisoners, halfway houses and major drug problems in that one Kensington neighborhood. It would be hard to find another square mile in the United States that felt as spiritually oppressed and hopeless. The heat and humidity were oppressive, and the noise from the elevated train 50 feet above the park was deafening. Fire trucks and police cars constantly drove by, blaring sirens and flashing lights. One night, I went out from the tent to see the park surrounded by police cars, as a hovering police helicopter shone a search light down on the area. It couldn't get much crazier than this.

The next year, a friend donated enough money to our ministry to purchase our own tent, chairs, tables, generators, lights and a trailer to haul everything. Over five years, we did fifteen separate events under that tent. People were drawn by the food and music or because they needed a place to nod off during their heroin stupor. Whatever the reason, they came. We got to know many of them quite well. Some would disappear, and return a couple of years later and tell us how they went into the tent stoned out of their minds but came out straight.

Hearing the stories from these men and women, many of whom were fathers and mothers, was heartwarming and encouraging. It gave us the hope that the vision would one day come true. Perhaps one of the people God touched in those meetings will be the person God will use to spark a great revival in the heart of our cities.

Some of the area's residents told us they looked for our blue and white tent because we weren't like all the rest that would come to the park. They said we were different, "Because you never yell at us." "They keep telling us we're going to hell," one man said, adding that one night he yelled back at them: "You don't need to tell me I am going to hell – I live in hell every day!"

The hardest time was from midnight to 6 a.m. We would leave a few men to guard the tent; it was a hard job and not for the faint-hearted. Our generator was stolen twice.

One fourth of July weekend, I (Rex) stood by the tent when a man came up to me, arms folded in front of him. He told me our friend had sent him over, and he wanted to know if I could go somewhere to talk. Suspicious of being drawn away by a stranger, I said, "Here is fine, and I have time. What's on your mind?"

"I told the guy over there that I was the one that stole your generator from the tent a couple of years ago and he told me I needed to talk to you," he said. I didn't reply, because there was more he needed to say and I didn't want to make it any easier for him. Finding the silence unbearable, he said, "Yes, I was the one that came that night and stole it. I needed some money and it was there so I took it." He continued to make small talk, about where he had gone and what he had done with the money, but to tell you the truth I wasn't much interested.

"What do you want? Do you want me to forgive you for stealing our generator?" I asked.

He swallowed a couple of times and replied, "Yeah, I want you to forgive me."

I looked him in the eye and said, "Then you are going to have to ask me to forgive you." He looked confused, so I continued. "You told me you took something that did not belong to you but that is just a statement of fact. You have not told me you were sorry or that you wanted to be forgiven."

He shuffled around for a couple of seconds. "What do I have to say?"

"You have to tell me you're sorry for taking the generator and ask me to forgive you."

He looked down. "This is harder than I thought it would be."

"It's not supposed to be easy," I said, "but doing what is right is often not the easiest thing to do."

He looked me in the eye. "I am sorry for taking your generator. Will you please forgive me?"

"Of course I forgive you," I said. "But let me pray for you." With that, I put my hand on his shoulder and prayed for him. After a while, he looked up and there were tears in his eyes. He softly thanked me and with tears running down his cheeks he walked through the crowd, up the stairs to the EL train.

One night a young girl sat on the curb. We could see the Holy Spirit was drawing her but we didn't get a chance to go over to her right away. Finally, she came to the tent and told us that she only wanted someone to tell her they loved her. We found out that she was 18 years old, on drugs, abused, and involved in prostitution.

Lois and a number of the women gathered around her and prayed for her, one after another. Afterwards, a local worker took her to a thrift shop to get her some clothes. After changing, she came back and said that she had never felt the love of God like this before. She said that when Lois and the others had prayed for her, she had the sensation of "pure liquid love flowing all over me."

Another night, a young woman came into the tent in very sad shape. The men who were watching the tent all night pointed her out to us when we arrived the next morning. They said they had a tough time getting her to keep her clothes on, which she tried to take off several times during the night. She was hooked on crack and shot up constantly. She had massive infections and open sores, and was also into mutilating herself. Lois and a friend ministered to her and did not give up on her throughout the weekend. They took care of her physical needs and fed her, as well as told her how much Jesus loved her and how He died for her and that she could have a new life. At one point, she prayed to have Jesus come in and take over her life and allowed Lois to comb and care for her long hair.

At the end of that round of meetings, Lois felt she could not leave without helping her get out of that situation. The young woman agreed to let an ambulance come and take her to a hospital. Our friend found out she stayed in the hospital two days and we lost contact with her and didn't hear anything about her for a long time.

Almost two years later, the young woman heard we were going to be back at the park for our annual fourth of July outreach and came to see us. She told us she had been completely clean for a year and a half and that she was happy and about to be married. She had her fiancé with her as well as her four-year-old son. She looked great and was five months pregnant! We could barely recognize her as the same person. She thanked us for helping her that day in the park and Lois prayed again with her, for her new life and for her new family. What a transformation that took place within that young woman because she accepted Jesus as Lord and Savior. Praise God! Praise Him that He encourages us to keep going and that we can make a difference when we love as He loves.

From time to time, a couple we knew, pastors from New Jersey, would stop in at the tent to help out on a Saturday. We introduced them to a woman who had a women's ministry five blocks away from the park. Two years later, the woman gave the building to them for a dollar and they left their church in New Jersey and started a church there. Finally, we had a place to send the people from the streets to be ministered to and discipled by people that had a heart after God. They continue to minister from the Gospel of Jesus Christ, and represent His love and His heart for the broken ones.

One Friday night, a person showed up around 6 o'clock, claiming to be an inspector from the city. He told us we were in violation of virtually every city code you could think of. We learned that when you get a permit from the parks department to put up a tent, it didn't mean you could actually put up a tent. It meant you had a place to put up a tent. Then you needed a tent permit, followed by an electrical permit. You had to install various exit signs. All food preparation had to be approved by the health department. And we needed to prove we had a million dollars of insurance.

The inspector said that our meetings had grown to where they were an event, and landed on the city's radar screen. In retrospect, some of the new things required to have the tent events were a pain but some did make it better. The best part was watching the interaction between our friend who introduced us to the area and the inspector. We were enthralled seeing these two go at it. It was vintage *Rocky* stuff. They went back and forth, our friend thinking it was a shake down and the inspector getting offended.

Hundreds of people helped us throughout the years we were at the park. When we went out and spoke at churches, we showed a video of what it was like and asked people to come down and help. People from all over the US came, including one couple from a farm in North Dakota. The woman, who had never experienced anything remotely like this, was beside herself worrying about what she should or shouldn't do. We told her not to worry, we would make sure she would be kept busy. She and her husband came early, helped us put up the tent and got everything ready. When she saw the people, she was so overcome with emotion and the Father's heart for them that she just cried and cried. She may have cried for the entire three days. That couple continued to either come once a year to help us personally or supported us financially.

Once, a man came up to me (Rex) and asked if I remembered him. I did, of course; it seemed like he was always at the tent when we had it up. This visit was different. He looked cleaner and healthier than I had ever seen him. It was a clean that surpassed just being clean on the outside – you could see he was cleaner on the inside as well.

"I used to come here every time you guys had the tent up," he said. "I would come with my friends, eat and listen, and then we would go on about our ways. But when I saw you down here today, I wanted you to know that my life has changed. I was listening and you guys made such an impact on me that it got me to thinking. I don't even drink soft drinks anymore. Nothing, I'm straight and doing well. I thought you should know."

I knew those words came straight from the Father to me because they pierced my heart. Maybe a cup of cold water, along with a hamburger and some hot dogs and heaps of love on the side, goes further than we will ever know. A lot of us never get to hear a testimony like that one. What we do does matter, and the things we say and the way in which we say it, is heard.

On another Friday night, a middle aged woman asked for

ice. It took us a while to find some, but when we did, we brought it over to her at a park bench, where she sat with a friend. She was very appreciative that someone had taken the time to do something for her. A few minutes later, one of the men with us chatted with her and her friend. They all stood up, so we went to see what was happening. She told us she had just been released from jail (where she had gotten saved), was homeless, and had liver cancer. Because of the pain, she said she couldn't stand up straight.

Our worker had prayed with her, and now she was standing without any pain. She was a little unsteady, as the presence and glory of God was all over her. She was speechless, tearful, amazed, relieved and thankful. We were all awestruck and told her that God had healed her because He loved her.

She said she had seen people say they were healed like this on the *700 Club*, but wasn't sure it was real – until it happened to her! God also healed her mind and emotions. She looked like a different person than the woman who just a few minutes ago was looking for some ice to chew on because of the pain. What a miracle! She found a place to stay that night and one of the local women let her use her shower to clean up. When we saw her the next day she looked like a new person. One of the local pastors made arrangements for her to get permanent housing.

One of the people that came to help us gave us this story about what she experienced as part of the outreach:

What a hot and muggy day! The tent is up; chairs and sound system are in place. Volunteers are unloading cases of food from the trailer to the tent via human conveyer system. Lots of plans – bag the groceries, worship, prayer, instructions to treat all with dignity and kindness. Share the love of Jesus! It sounds simple to do but a lot of planning goes into a day like this and lots of prayer!

After helping pass out the bags of groceries to the homeless and the needy, we had opportunity for each to receive prayer and to share our love by listening and telling each of God's love. We encouraged each one to come back for the picnic at 3 PM or to stay under the cool tent and enjoy the great music and singing.

As soon as the huge grill was set up out under a big tree, lots of people from the street were watching curiously. The burgers and hot dogs were loaded onto the grill. What an aroma in the air! We began serving them quickly as they came off the grill, along with pasta salad, chips, homemade cupcakes with sprinkles (Boy, they are going fast, first choice for most!), and lots of other goodies too. What a joy to joke and laugh with everyone! After about two hours serving, another volunteer relieved me so I could get in line to get food for myself. The line was still out past the big shade tree where the grill was set up. As I stood at the end of the line, a young man came up to me and said, "What's going on here? What is this?"

"It's a picnic! It's free!" I said. I noticed how well dressed he was and very polite and encouraged him to join us. As we stood in line together, he asked more questions. Is it a church event? (He could hear the wonderful music under the tent.) What church, what's the name? I, jokingly, explained that it was Christians coming together, not churches – no signs, just feeding anyone who wanted to come. After finding out that he was just on his way to the EL train roaring above us, we got our food and I invited him to sit and join us. He sat in the front, right up near the microphone, and

ate while enjoying the music. We continued to chat, as he noticed the homeless and the prostitutes all around us. We were all eating together and he was taking it all in very curiously.

A young pastor began to share his story of when God became "real" to him. It was a message from his heart and the quiet in the tent attested to that. After him was a young woman who shared that Jesus was the "answer" to everyone's questions. The young man finished eating but sat fixed to his chair. The musicians came back and began singing again and that's when it happened!

"Jesus loves me, this I know, for the Bible tells me so." You know the song – we all learned it in Sunday school. Everyone that's ever been to vacation Bible school or been raised in a Christian church remembers this song! I glanced over to my right and tears were streaming down his cheeks. I reached over and put my hand on his arm and patted it and he put his hand on mine. Nothing needed to be said. This tent was here for ALL the "lost."

I know I did not see what I saw in the dream fully materialize while we were in the heart of Philadelphia. Perhaps it's for later and maybe for someone that was touched at one of the meetings. I do know that you can't wait for a dream to come true – you must put feet to it. You must actively pursue it. We did and made some incredible memories that will stay with us forever. Even now, I vividly recall scenes of men and women coming up and asking for prayer and the power of God hitting them. Down they would go into the grass, laying there for hours as the love of God poured into them and over them. As one prostitute said, "I used to be able to make $500 to $700 a day here before everyone started praying. Now Marilyn Monroe herself couldn't make a living!"

WHEN THE FIRE FALLS

Chapter 12

THE GOODNESS OF GOD

The Night The Glory Fell!

I (Rex) awoke in the middle of the night as waves of doubt and fear rolled over me. Thoughts of "Who did I think I was anyway?" bombarded me. "Why did I think that I had anything to offer to these people? Why don't I just go home!" I was crippled with fear, but something in that last statement about giving up and going home seemed too familiar. Once again, Satan had overplayed his hand and I recognized the voice of the enemy. A resolve came back into my heart and spirit as I awakened to what was happening. I rebuked the demonic spirit and fell back into a deep and peaceful sleep. The next morning, I found out that Lois had been going through the same series of dreams and accusations and had come to the same conclusion as me. Even the words the enemy used were similar.

We got ready for breakfast, and I couldn't help but think back to the day before and our flight into Hartford. We had just been told by the flight attendants to prepare for landing, when I noticed Lois was holding her jaw in pain. She was experiencing incredibly painful aches in her lower front teeth. The pain came out of nowhere and increased to such intensity that, as we waited for our baggage, we thought we might go and find a dentist. The pastor picking us up saw the pain on Lois's face and was very concerned.

As we drove the 45 minutes to where we would stay, and talked about whether or not we should find a dentist or go straight to a hospital emergency room. The pain came on so fast and escalated at such an alarming rate that it boggled our minds. Lois moaned as the waves of pain came upon her.

It took us a long time – too long – before we came to the conclusion that we should pray. We came against any spirit of affliction that may have attached itself to Lois, bound it, canceled its assignment and commanded it to leave. Within seconds, almost 90 per cent of the pain had subsided and Lois felt she would be all right. As we marveled at how quickly God had touched Lois, the pastor told us that the largest witches coven in the northeastern United States was only a half mile from the church and he was sure they were aware we were coming into the area as he had advertised the meetings all around town.

Throughout our time in the Hartford suburb of Canton, Lois would occasionally feel pain in her teeth. But as the wheels of the plane lifted off the ground and Connecticut disappeared behind us, all remnants of pain left and never returned.

I didn't get off scot-free. When we arrived at the church to set up a product table, I reached into the trunk of the pastor's car for a small box of training manuals. I felt excruciating pain in my lower back and could not bend over at all. I have had back pain before but this was in a much lower place than where it would usually occur and it was bad. From that time on, we knew we were under attack and felt like we had a big target painted on our heads.

We came to train the congregation on the subjects of healing, deliverance and how to implement words of knowledge. There were about 300 people present in a picturesque, two century old church that looked like it came right out of a Norman Rockwell painting. The community's main road split and went around the church, making it the focal point of the town. The inside was beautiful with stained glass windows and a balcony around three sides of the sanctuary.

People from five churches came to the Canton meetings, a third of them being United Methodist, a third from the home Congregational Church, and the rest solid Evangelicals. There was not a charismatic in sight. The crowd was older, too - no teenagers, no twentysomethings. The average age had to be 60 years old.

They were not used to the manifestations of the Holy Spirit and had no idea of spiritual terms such as being slain in the spirit or impartation by the laying on of hands. I would be amazed if any of them had ever watched a Benny Hinn crusade on television or anything that would resemble one.

Yet the training went well. After each of the sessions, we had a clinic time where they practiced the things they had been taught. Several times the pastor came to us totally amazed, telling us he had been there for a decade and never seen some of these people ever pray. He was even more amazed when it came to receiving and giving words of knowledge for healing. It seemed as if everyone came forward and participated, which resulted in some incredible healings. Everything presented had been done with the underpinning of a solid Biblical approach. We had not prayed for anyone ourselves, so no one had fallen down or been affected in any unusual manner by what was happening.

The Saturday evening healing service was open to the community. We wanted the people we had trained to put into practice what they had learned during the previous day and a half. They were our ministry team. Little did we realize that we were about to enter into something supernaturally awesome in power and mercy. We have seen many things but we never witnessed anything, before or since, that was so full of God's grace and overwhelming presence. Father God really had a deep affection for the people present; we have never witnessed the power of the Holy Spirit come upon people so gently as that night.

I (Lois) and a number of others, mainly women, went into a separate room in the back of the church to intercede for the meeting. Our hearts were sincere, asking God to bring healing to His people. The power of God came in that prayer time and I interceded passionately for the fire of God to fall in the meeting. We prayed for the Lord to come with His presence and capture the people with His amazing love and power. We asked Him to save any that did not know Him, to heal them, and to bring freedom to His people.

The meeting started. We got lost in the worship provided by a few charismatics they had found in town. To be honest, we weren't entirely sure how to proceed. In our previous talks with the pastor we told him a general plan but also let him know that all of it could change. We had to wait and see. Originally, I (Rex) planned to preach a short message, explain what words of knowledge were, and then let our fledgling ministry team come and give words of knowledge for healing.

That all changed when we asked the people present to raise their hands if they were here for the first time. Only ten people raised their hands, which meant that the other 300 had all gone through the training. It didn't seem practical for them to come forward and give words of knowledge especially after they had just done so a few hours before.

Lois and I gave ten words of knowledge to see what would happen. During the next ten minutes or so, a dozen people stood for the words we gave and were healed.

I was about to start my message when Lois came toward me. I gave her the microphone and Lois asked all those who had been diagnosed with any terminal disease, and had only six months or less to live, to come forward, as she felt the Lord wanted her to pray for them. Seven people, without hesitation, got up out of their chairs and came for prayer. I remember thinking that I was glad she put a time limit of six months on her request because as old as this group was, we could have been flooded with people coming forward for healing.

Lois motioned for them to come to one side of the sanctuary and prayed for them, which gave me the opportunity to begin the message. I started my sermon and watched out of the corner of my eye as Lois lifted her hand to pray for the first person. They fell to the floor, overcome by the presence of God and the Holy Spirit's touch. An entire section of the church, comprised of one hundred United Methodists sitting together, turned their heads in perfect unison to look. Their eyes bulged and their mouths opened wide. They had never seen anything like that before.

The one hundred Congregationalists, not to be outdone, followed suit, turning their heads to watch Lois pray for the people who had come forward. Within the next few minutes, all seven of the people that had come up for prayer were laying on the floor. As I watched what was happening I knew it would be useless for me to continue as none of the people were interested in hearing the message. They were glued to Lois and what was going on over on the side of the sanctuary.

I tried to keep them focused with some stories, knowing it would be foolish to start the message as hardly anyone was listening. After a while, they came around, their mouths and eyes went back to their normal positions, and I again tried to preach my message on revival.

Finishing the sermon, I asked if anyone wanted to come forward for prayer and to receive a fresh touch from God. I was stunned when all 300 people got up from their pews and came forward en masse. This was a physical problem; the structure of a congregational church does not give anyone room for ministry. There was only about four feet of space between the first pew and the picket fence that separated the people from the minister. The speaker only had a small platform to stand on and no room to roam. Behind the pulpit were four steps that rose to a small choir platform. A grand piano sat on the right side and an organ on the left. There was virtually no room to pray for people.

Earlier, Lois had asked the pastor if we could take everyone into the back room fellowship hall, which was behind the worship team. It was just fifteen feet from the pulpit to the hall. The pastor told us that although he would like to think that people would get touched and be slain in the spirit, he just didn't think that would ever happen in Canton. He had been on a trip to Brazil and to some of Randy Clark's meetings, so he knew what to expect in meetings.

As the people crowded toward us, we saw some of them had managed to squeeze into the small space between the front row and stage. They all looked like our 80-year-old mothers; most of the congregation was older than we were. It was like praying for a gathering of grandparents. They were so sweet; they looked up at us and we were suddenly overwhelmed with our Father's deep compassion for them. We lifted our hands to pray and the first woman wilted and collapsed to the floor. We just looked at the next four and with a slight wave of our hand, they ever so gently slipped quietly onto the ground. They had not fallen backward, they simply wilted in His presence, and now rested on the floor. They were totally overcome by the Holy Spirit, as if they were in the most deep and peaceful sleep.

The pastor's eyes and mouth fell wide open in amazement at the women that were now lying so peacefully at his feet. "Do you think it would be alright to take them into the fellowship hall where we would have more room?" we asked. "Yes, yes, I believe that would be alright," he said.

We told everyone to follow us into the fellowship hall for prayer. They crowded into the room, and we asked them to line up in rows with about eight feet between each row. The pastor picked eight of the youngest and healthiest men to assist us, which meant anyone in their fifties. I (Rex) jumped up on a chair in front and gave a few instructions on how to receive prayer. I also gave brief instructions to the catchers just in case they fell, so no one would be hurt. There were some older and fragile saints of God there.

I came off the chair and looked to see whom the Holy Spirit rested upon. We could see Him moving on the hearts of people and as we came up to the first line, they fell over together, six or eight of them at a time. It was as if they simply wilted and fainted under the anointing. Within a few minutes, sixty people were out on the floor. Not long after that, nearly everyone else was overwhelmed with His presence and down as well.

There was not a noisy or demonstrative manifestation on anyone present – no crying, no laughing, no shaking, no jerking. Just the most peaceful countenance on their faces. They were not down for a couple of minutes and then jumping to their feet; these people experienced Him in a lengthy, profound encounter. Many of them laid there for more than half an hour.

Later, Lois had several of them come to her. "I just never knew how much Jesus loved me. Do you think we could do that again sometime?" they said. Lois was so moved with compassion for them that she would put her hand out and again the presence of God would flood them and down they would go.

We have never seen, before or since, such an outpouring of the sweetness of God as the one we witnessed that night. Any violent or noisy manifestation could have caused concern; God came in a sovereign visitation that was manifested in His kindness and in His unfathomable gentle and tender love for them all.

We met with the pastor later and explained to him the special grace that we knew was on the meeting. We told him it was the hunger for more of God that led pastors like John Arnott of Toronto and John Kilpatrick of Brownsville to keep Randy Clark and Steve Hill at their churches far past the time the meetings were due to close. Both of these pastors noticed something special about the meetings and that it was the time of visitation they had been seeking.

Many churches have prayed for an outpouring of His presence and for revival to come, but either did not recognize it or act upon what He brought to them. They let it slip through their fingers. If the pastors in Toronto or Brownsville had not recognized what was happening in their midst, they would be doing now what they had previously been doing and most likely Randy Clark would still be pastoring a small church in St. Louis, and Steve Hill would still be doing small evangelistic meetings.

"I never realized how much responsibility this puts on us as senior pastors," the pastor said.

"That's true," I replied. "The responsibility to hear from God and make a decision is up to you. All I can do is let you know that something unique has happened tonight, something very special that we have never experienced before."

The pastor could not make the decision to have us stay any longer or continue the meetings, so we left as scheduled the next day. We found out shortly afterward that two men, one who attended all the meetings except Saturday evening and another man who never came to the meetings at all, tried to have the pastor removed. Sad as it is, two men worked to discourage and confuse those dear saints who had such an amazing and unforgettable visitation of His great love and presence. However, we know that just as we have never been the same since He touched us and overwhelmed us with His presence, they also will never be the same. None who were there will forget the night the glory cloud came to Canton, Connecticut.

WHEN THE FIRE FALLS

Chapter 13

DOUBTS AND WONDERINGS

Sometimes You Just Got To Wonder

In case you think what we experienced was idyllic, you should know we too had our times of doubt. Just because you shake, rattle and roll does not mean you do not wake up in the morning and doubt what you experienced. There are also plenty of people that are happy to throw water on any fire and for any reason.

Often times, misunderstandings come out of simple miscommunication. If we would just take the time to ask another person what they meant when they said a specific thing, many misunderstandings would be avoided. One day I (Rex) pulled into the church to talk with the pastor for a few minutes. The church secretary told me he was busy with a couple, but would be done soon. I waited in the sanctuary, listening to the worship music playing. The pastor's office door opened and out came the couple. I recognized them and watched as they came around the sanctuary to where I sat.

The husband started the conversation. "I just want you to know we talked with the pastor and we forgive you." I was surprised, as I couldn't think of anything I needed their forgiveness for.

"Thank you but what did I do?" I replied.

"One day when you prayed for my wife you repeatedly told her to fall. But we forgive you for doing that," he said. My mind raced a mile a minute trying to think of when and where this could possibly have happened. As I stood and thanked them for forgiving me, the Lord reminded me of the moment.

The couple were part of the church's ministry team and before every Thursday evening service, we prayed in a separate room. We had just returned from another trip to Kelowna where the worship leader, David Ruis, had taught the song, *Let the Fire Fall in this Room*. I remember that as I prayed for the wife, the song was on my mind, and I said, "Let the fire fall, let it fall, let it fall, let it fall." They assumed I was telling her to fall, which was something I would never do. I didn't try to correct them. I knew it wasn't worth it, so I thanked them again and watched as they left. I cautioned myself to watch what I prayed over people from that moment on.

On another occasion, we returned home late from yet another Sunday night meeting, and sat up for many hours, talking about whether or not we should try to get our lives back to some form of normalcy. We had been on quite the roller coaster of emotions over the past few months because of all that happened following our touch from God. We tried to sort everything out in our minds. God had definitely touched us and He was powerfully using us, but it came with a cost. Some of our closest friends didn't understand and stayed away from us. It hurt.

We received different dreams and impressions within our spirits almost every night while we slept. Almost in unison, the

Holy Spirit would bring to our minds a specific individual or couple that He wanted us to contact. When we woke in the morning, one of us would mention someone's name and it would be the same name the other person had. We recognized that God wanted us to minister to them, so we would call and invite them over to our home.

When they came, God faithfully gave us a word for them, and as we prayed over them, the power of God came and down they would go, often for quite an extended period. It became almost a nightly experience for our family to have people over and have them end up on the floor, experiencing His love and transformation as they spent time in His presence.

Some of the biggest changes we experienced were in our personal habits. For ten years, I (Rex) had faithfully written down everything that happened on a daily basis. Almost everything I recorded had to do with our business and found its way into my little black book. I had a big stack of these books (in fact, we still have them). But when God came so powerfully all of that changed. My focus in life shifted dramatically and I just had no interest in doing that anymore. In fact, I lost my heart to grow the business. Something had transformed within me that was so wonderful that it totally captured and refocused my heart, mind and spirit.

The presence of God was so powerfully on us during that first year that we often shook during the day and night. Many times we were awakened at night with what we could only describe as the kisses from God upon us. We would hear the other cry out, "Oh Jesus, Jesus," and we would both tremble and often shake violently. We wondered at times if we were ever going to get a full night's rest without being awakened by His presence. During the day, at work, in the grocery store or mowing the lawn, the presence of God would come upon us. It was as if we had been arrested by the Holy Spirit and He was letting us know that we were no longer in charge of our lives.

For more than three years, I (Rex) was an elder and on the governing board of the church. As I think back over all the meetings I was a part of, I cannot remember a time when the board was not in total agreement. The harmony, love and respect each of us had for the others was amazing. However, that changed once revival came to the church. One of our most influential elders retired from the board a month before the revival came. He often dealt with issues of low self-esteem, and told me that he felt that God had to get him out of the way so that the revival could happen. He was highly respected by all within the church and it became an issue to many when this man kept his distance from the revival, even though his wife had come to Kelowna with us and been powerfully touched.

Another elder at the church constantly opposed the move of God and often ridiculed me during the elders meetings. He told me one day, "How can this be God if you say your heart isn't in your business anymore? Why would God do that?" This sent me into a tailspin of emotional thoughts. It took me several days to sort through it all and come to any conclusion. I was well aware that my heart was not in my work anymore so I played over the events that took place the previous day when I went to the lumberyard to pick up materials. Normally it would take me only an hour to order and load up the materials. Now it took me much longer, as I found myself constantly surrounded by people that were asking me questions about God. Before, I would hardly, if ever, share anything about God. Now people were coming up to me asking me questions about the meetings and what was happening to me. The workers helping me load material were very interested in what was happening and wanted to hear the stories. I really felt the presence of God was drawing them to ask questions of me. I had become a part of an event that was worthy of an explanation.

I also thought about when I went to pick up some steel for one of our jobs. Again, I found myself surrounded in the back by the yardmen asking me about God. Mormons and non-believers crowded around as I told them story after story of what God was doing. I realized the reason I was not getting much done at work was because I was spending so much time answering questions about what God was doing. Even after driving up on the job site, I sometimes found myself sitting in my pickup truck as the presence of God swept over me.

One day, as I waited at a red light, cars came from the opposite turn lane and passed right in front of me. I felt as if each person looked directly at me. As I looked at them, I sensed that I was peering right into their souls and I saw the need for God in their lives. I felt His love for them and couldn't help it when tears streamed down my face. This was not the only occasion that God revealed to me His heart for the lost. I never understood what was happening to me on those occasions but it was an amazing experience.

THROWN IN THE FIERY FURNACE

It was in the middle of all this that we came home that Sunday night from church and wondered if we should back out of things for a while. We wanted some normalcy back in our lives. After talking it over, we decided we should step out of the forefront of this move in our church. Feeling we had settled the issue, we went to sleep.

Around midnight, we were both awakened by the fiery presence of God. Looking at the numbers on the clock, we saw it was exactly twelve. Immediately, my body began to experience bolts of power and I (Rex) went from lying on my back to sitting upright in bed and then back down again. Lois exclaimed that she felt like she was burning up under the intense fire of God's presence. For close to three hours, this strange phenomenon overwhelmed us. It wouldn't stop. We couldn't figure out what was happening to us. We felt like we were under the heat lamp and power of God's presence. It was hard to even speak, although we were both noisy with the sound that came forth as wave after wave of the Holy Spirit washed over us.

"I guess He doesn't agree that we should stop," Lois said afterward. We recommitted ourselves to the plans He had designed for our lives. We both knew God had plans beyond our understanding and that they didn't include us backing down from what He wanted.

DISCOURAGED AND CONFUSED

As we talked about what happened that night, we wondered why we had felt like backing off from how God was using us. We had been going through a time of discouragement, tiredness, and at times just wanted to give up. We were challenged by a book written by Cindy Jacobs, which said, "If you are feeling confusion, heaviness and discouragement in your ministry you may be having someone praying manipulative prayers over you." She said that sometimes, well-intentioned Christians pray prayers against what you are doing because they feel it's what God wants to happen. They may say they love you but think you're on the wrong track and pray 'soulish' prayers, which are in reality, witchcraft prayers designed to manipulate you.

Cindy recommended this prayer in her book, *Possessing the Gates of the Enemy*: "Father, in the name of Jesus, I now break the power of every word prayed for me that is contrary to Your will for my life. I thank You now that all bondage is broken from any manipulating prayers." We agreed this could be a very real cause for why we felt so tired and discouraged. We held hands and prayed the prayer together.

Within a few hours, our phone rang. It was a friend from church who had been to our home many times and who Lois had personally counseled. She wanted to talk to us, so we invited her over to the house the next day for lunch.

The next day, we had a good lunch and a great conversation, and then she opened up. She told us that the day before, about a half hour before she called us, she felt a heavy conviction come upon her about what she had been doing. Even though she personally liked what was happening at the church, many of her friends were not as enthused. They were quite concerned and it had become an issue with her. She knew we meant well, but felt we were unable to see the effects our actions were having on the church. She came to ask us to forgive her, because the Holy Spirit had convicted her that her prayers, that we would become tired and discouraged in being a part of this move of God, were not from Him. She said it wasn't personal; we were highly visible leaders and she thought it was God's will that she pray for us in this way. The sad thing is she actually thought she was doing the right thing until the Holy Spirit convicted her the previous day and she knew she had to call us and repent. We had her repent for her prayers, and we hugged and she left. Our tiredness and discouragement left as well. From that day on, we have continued to say Cindy's prayer over our lives on a regular basis.

This disconnect from some of our friends was difficult. Within a few months of the beginning of the outpouring in our lives, I (Lois) felt continually captured by Him and astounded by His love and power. There really were very few minutes of the day or night that I did not sense and know His manifest presence in my life.

What I could not understand was that some of our best friends at church were unhappy with what God was doing. They told us if this was truly God, He would bring total unity in the church. This was not happening. In fact, some were so upset over the revival that they would rather not have it than the problems it brought. I love peace and, at that time, I would do most anything to avoid confrontation or any form of discord in the church. The thought that we were causing disruption or being misunderstood was difficult for me to grasp.

To pray about this, I went down into our basement and soon found myself in heavy travail and intercession to know God's will for our lives and to understand what He was doing. Within one hour of starting, I received a phone call from a woman in our church that had never called us before – and very few times, if ever, since.

"Lois," she said, "I was praying just a little while ago about what God is doing in the church and with me personally. He gave me a specific Scripture and He told me to call you and tell you that this Scripture is to be given to you in answer to your questions. It is Isaiah 55."

Isaiah 55:8 ministered particularly during those first months – *"For My thoughts are not your thoughts, nor are your ways My ways says the Lord. For as the heavens are higher than the earth, so are My ways higher than your ways, and My thoughts than your thoughts."* Later, we saw Isaiah 55:5 come to pass in our life, *"Surely you shall call a nation you do not know. And nations who do not know you shall run to you, Because of the Lord your God and the Holy One of Israel; for He has glorified you."*

His ways are higher than our ways. Jesus is the Son of God. God came in the flesh as Jesus Christ, the Lamb slain for the atonement of our sin. He is the Way and the Truth and the Life and no one comes to the Father except through Him. His ways are so far beyond our human thinking that He sent His only Son that we could be saved! All praise and honor and glory are given to Him that He might use us as His vessels in a broken and hurting world. And as we continue to say "yes" to His plan for our lives, there will be some people, even in the church, that do not understand.

WHEN THE FIRE FALLS

Chapter 14

IF IT WALKS LIKE A DUCK...

Strange Fire

"Who struck you violently across your face?" I (Rex) asked the woman. Her eyes rolled back in her head leaving only the whites showing. Her entire body trembled and she groaned – a sad and mournful sound that grew louder and louder. It was close to 1 a.m. and I was in Vallejo, California, at a church ministering. It was the final night of meetings and I was tired. The plane ride out of San Francisco was scheduled for six in the morning and I knew that even if we left for the hotel immediately, I would only get a couple of hours sleep before I would be picked up for the ride to the airport.

It always seems to happen this way: the most desperate and hurting people come to you at the end of the meetings when you are exhausted and ready to leave. An hour earlier, the woman had come to me with a question. "When you prayed for me, I felt the presence of God, but then I felt something crawling along the side of my face," she said. "Do you think that was God?"

I prayed for her and noticed that God was touching her but I wasn't aware of anything else happening. "I have heard a lot of words used to describe the attributes of God when He comes upon a person: gentleness, love, compassion, joy, peace – but feeling 'something crawling along the side of your face' is not one of them," I said.

I asked the Holy Spirit to come and within a short time, her countenance relaxed and the peace of God came over her. I left her there and prayed for several other people that were waiting and, after a while, I came back to her. I asked her how she felt and she said the same thing had happened. She felt the presence of the Lord and then a sensation as if something was crawling on her face. I told her that something was happening to her that definitely was not of God and, learning that this was her home church, I suggested she make an appointment with the pastor to go through counseling, which she agreed to do.

I was only a couple of steps away from her when I suddenly turned and out of my mouth tumbled the words, "Who struck you violently across your face?" I was just as shocked at the force of the words as she was, but my reaction was much different than hers. She went into a full-blown demonic manifestation, which worsened by the second. If I didn't do something immediately she was going to be on the floor and it was not going to be good. I was familiar with this kind of situation as it had happened before. I knew what to do.

I took hold of her hands to stop her from falling to the floor. Because her name was on her name badge, I could communicate with her and bring her back to herself. In a normal, but firm, tone, I commanded the demon to submit in the name of Jesus. I called her name, telling her that Jesus was here, I was here, and everything was going to be all right. It took several times of commanding the demon to submit and calling out her name for the hold on the woman to be released, but I soon had her back. Her eyes returned to their normal position and though she was shaken, she was in control of herself.

I asked again who had struck her violently across the face. She said she had just left a bitter and abusive marriage where her husband had physically slapped and punched her in the face. I asked if she still thought that making an appointment with the pastor for some counseling was a good idea, and she nodded yes. We then walked over to the pastor and set up an appointment. The more severe and out of control the demonic manifestation is, the more the person recognizes that they truly are not in command and something else very evil has control in their life. Once they realize this, they almost always want to be set free. It is through Jesus Christ and in His power and authority they find freedom and are made whole. He pours out His love and heals our brokenness and wounds.

LEARNING THROUGH DESPERATION

When we first traveled with Randy, we were already aware of the demonic and how to set people free. But we still had a lot to learn. I (Rex) had personally gone through a sovereign deliverance years before so we had no doubt demons were real and could influence people. However, we did not realize that traveling with Randy would put us on the front lines of doing deliverance. Even when we were with people who were more knowledgeable and who really wanted to do deliverance, they still wanted us to be there. Note the phrase, "who really wanted to do deliverance," and you will understand our hesitancy.

In the early days with Randy, it was not uncommon that it

would be just the three of us who ministered. We did not take teams on all of the trips we were on, even though the crowds we ministered to could number as many as 3,000. Many times, we did not see each other for hours, as we would be in different parts of a building praying for people.

In one meeting, they took me (Rex) downstairs, leaving Randy upstairs in the sanctuary. The basement was as large as the meeting room upstairs. The doors burst open on the other side of the room and close to a thousand people streamed in, filling the room. It was quite a sight and very sobering to think all those people wanted to receive prayer from you.

With my interpreter by my side, I went from one person to the next, praying as quickly as I could. For most of them, a simple touch of the hand upon their heads or shoulder was enough and down they fell. After an hour, I made it to a corner of the room and prayed for a young woman in her early twenties. As I raised my hand to pray for her, a moan like a siren came out of her and intensified in volume as I kept my hand up. Recognizing this was a spiritual problem, I removed my hand and went to pray for the next person in line. I kept praying for people and every now and then, I would extend my hand towards her and out would come that mournful sound.

Another rush of people crowded in; I turned and she was right there in front of me. Her eyes rolled back in her head and she frothed at the mouth. Down to the floor she went, shaking uncontrollably. Without taking my eyes off her, I asked the interpreter to find out what her name was. My interpreter bolted across the room and with one last look over his shoulder, he disappeared through the door and up the stairs. He left! My interpreter had fled the scene! I turned around and saw at least a hundred people that I could not communicate with, looking at me, then at the girl on the floor, and expecting me to do something.

I looked at them and, in desperation, asked them what her name was. I said, "My name Rex, what is her name?" motioning at the girl. Finally someone understood and grabbed my arm and said, "Julianna."

I got down on my knees next to her and commanded the demon to submit in the name of Jesus. I then said, "Julianna, Jesus loves you, can you say the name of Jesus? Say Jesus." I only knew enough Portuguese to know the name of Jesus, but slowly her lips moved and she said His precious name, over and over, louder and louder. She opened her eyes and they were back to normal. Her shaking stopped and we were able to get her back on her feet. Of course, I had no interpreter to explain anything to her nor take her through deliverance, as the crowds again demanded that I pray for them.

To get an individual back in control of themselves once they demonically manifest, you must allow love to rule your actions. The person is more shocked than you realize, and the louder you shout at them, the more power you give the demon. Never shout at a demon nor try to find out its name. The demon is the least of your concerns – your focus is on the person and what they have done, or what has been done to them by others, to allow this entity to harass them. That is why we command the demon to submit in the name of Jesus.

There is no need to yell to make them submit. Never talk to a demon, except in the rarest instances and only for the purpose of expulsion. Remember, to converse with them is bordering on mediumship, which is strictly forbidden by God. They are liars anyway; demons will do anything they can to prolong their stay in a human being. In the name of Jesus and in His power and authority, command them to stop what they are doing and to not hurt or embarrass the individual. You may have to repeat this statement over and over in the process, but they must submit.

Constantly reassure the person that you are not going to leave them in this state. Tell them Jesus loves them so much and that He has sent you here to help them be set free and that you're going to help them through this. In most cases, this is the first time they have physically manifested and they are often terrified. If they happen to open their eyes and see that you are more fearful than they are, or that you are yelling at them to submit, they can conclude that they are the ones who are hideous, not the demon. This will cause them to fall further under demonic control. You must command the demon to submit while still conveying to the person that they are loved and that you will never leave them in this situation.

We have had people so under the power of the demonic spirit that they couldn't even speak. We told them to "think" the name of Jesus, and soon they were able to whisper His name and finally speak out loud, "Jesus." When they are back in control, ask them two things. First, see if they realize that something has gained spiritual control over their life and then ask them if they want to be set free. Second, ask if they know Jesus Christ as their Savior and Lord and explain that they must be saved to be set free and stay free. Almost always, we lead them in a prayer to recommit their lives to Jesus, even if they say they are already Christians.

The more severe the demonic manifestation, the more anxious the person is to get rid of it. It's one thing to think you just have a bad habit or that this is just how your family is, but when you personally witness a slimy demon that can override your ability to be in control, it scares the dickens out of you and you are more than willing to never have that happen again.

SLOUGH, ENGLAND

Across the room, we heard a scream and saw two of our friends, with the help of others, carrying a girl out of the meeting. We were in Slough, England, where we were experiencing one of the most severe outbreaks of demonic manifestations that we had ever seen in one place. The crazy thing is we were in a church where people were supposed to already know Jesus as their Savior.

The crowd parted so we could make our way over. Our friend's shirt, half tucked in, was ripped open with half the buttons missing. His hair was a mess, but his hold on the girl was firm, as were the others that helped. His wife followed, holding a handkerchief around her bleeding thumb, which had been bitten to the bone. As our friend went by, he looked over his shoulder at us and said, "We got ours, you get your own." I was more than willing to let him have all of them, but the pastor insisted we go with them to make sure things were done right.

We helped for half an hour, until we were sure the young woman was going to be all right. Returning to the meeting, we prayed for people again when another commotion started – another demonic manifestation. People yelled at both the demon and the person thrashing on the floor; again, the pastor asked us to help. We cut through a group of people just to get to him, and instructed everyone to back away and to leave him alone. We commanded the demon to submit in the name of Jesus and the person was back on his feet in just a few minutes. We dislike the demonic so much that we will do anything to stop what it is doing and bring the person back into their right mind. Both of us have learned to respond quickly and with God's authority to prevent the individual from being hurt and humiliated. It is not Godly to allow the demonic to harm or bring attention to itself with a suffering person at risk. Each of us needs to know what to do, and the authority He has given us, to command demons to submit.

The first time we encountered a demonic manifestation, it was in one of our small groups back in the 1980s. We had just taught on the demonic and we always followed a time of teaching by asking the Holy Spirit to come and show us anything further that we needed to know. Being in charge of the meeting, I waited a few moments before opening my eyes and as I looked around, I noticed a woman jerking her head from side to side. I jumped out of my chair, took her head in my hands, and told her to open her eyes. As she did, her eyes rolled back – only the whites were showing. My first thought was not the greatest one I've ever had: "Okay, now just have her close her eyes and go sit down like you didn't see anything."

We ministered to the woman for quite a while and helped deliver her of many things, but it was obvious that there was one spirit we couldn't cast out because she wasn't telling us the full truth. We found out later she had been involved in an adulterous affair and was unwilling to reveal it and repent. There was nothing we could do so we ended the session. Despite that, she came every now and then to our weekly meeting and sometimes demonically manifested. We would look her in the eyes and say, "Stop it." She usually shook her head a couple of times, and then her eyes refocused and she would be all right for the rest of the meeting.

RANDY DOES CARLOS ANNACONDIA STYLE OF DELIVERANCE

Early in our time with Randy, he followed the pattern that Carlos Annacondia used in the Argentina revival. Randy had learned from Carlos and used the same method Carlos used. During ministry time, Randy asked people to come forward – those who had just been saved, those who had recommitted their lives to Jesus, those who were under any addictions, those who knew they were oppressed by the enemy, or those battling with emotional problems. This drew many people to the front. Randy would then speak out with authority, coming against sexual sins (naming them specifically), substance abuse (naming them), and other sins, as the Lord led. When he did this, people demonically manifested, we pointed them out, and ushers took them to a separate room where trained people ministered to them. It was great in theory, but in practice we never seemed to have enough trained people to help them all, so this meant everyone had plenty to do. The main job was to keep the demons quiet because when one acted up, it got all the other demons manifesting. They were like animals – when one dog barked, others joined.

One of our jobs was to stand on the platform beside Randy when he called out the sins. We were the pointers, letting ushers know who needed to be helped to the other room.

After a while, we could pick out of a crowd 90 per cent of those who would manifest; just by their countenance and demeanor. We found that if a person could not make eye contact and appeared to be abnormally burdened or troubled, they usually had a demonic problem. We also got better at figuring out who might be ready to vomit so we could command the demon to submit, thus stopping the demon from further embarrassing the individual and, of course, creating quite a mess.

A Christian cannot be possessed by a demon. We have been purchased by the blood of Jesus, making it is impossible for us to be totally under demonic control or possessed. However, a Christian can be under bondage to a demonic spirit. We have learned there are stages that a person often goes through, leading them to be influenced demonically and then demonically manifest. First comes experimentation, which can open a person up to consciously making a choice to sin again. That choice can become a habit, and a habit left unchecked will put a person into bondage to sin. The more an individual is in bondage, the more likely they will experience being demonically oppressed, which changes their countenance and the direction of their life to bring even more deception and destruction. Finally, if they are not saved, it can lead to being totally possessed by Satan.

Understanding the degrees that sin takes an individual down a slippery path of destruction is vital. It helps you to correctly recognize the manifestation someone is exhibiting so that you can lead them into freedom. That is why so many people who have habits do not recognize it as being a problem. It hasn't reached the point where the manifestation has overridden their conscious effort to stop. However, once the demon comes in and takes over, the person sees they are not in control and are more apt to want to be free. If you want to see if a person has a habit just remember this line: "I can quit anytime I want to – I just don't want to quit now." That line is typically used by someone that has a habit they cannot control. If you see their countenance change when they are under the influence of that habit, you know they are battling spiritual oppression. The more a person is into a habit and oppressed, the greater the demonic manifestation.

That said, not everyone who manifests demonically does so because of their own choice to sin. We have ministered to many people who were hurt or abused by others. It had nothing to do with their personal decisions; it was beyond their control. These cases mainly involve sexual defilement or abuse. We have also seen those who have suffered severe trauma from incidents or accidents, which allowed a demon of fear to enter them. This is often tied to their childhood, usually from witnessing extreme violence or abuse. It is never for us to judge an individual when they manifest demonically but to act quickly and demonstrate His love to the broken ones and the captives.

After all of these experiences ministering to the demonically oppressed, we have no doubt that we live in a spiritual world and that Satan is both real and knows his time is short. We marvel at the unfathomable and faithful love of our Lord and we are humbled to be His vessels to bring salvation, healing and deliverance to those He has planned ahead of time for us to minister to. Satan is not an equal match for our Lord. God far exceeds the powers of the evil one. It is only in Jesus' power and authority that we are victorious.

WHEN THE FIRE FALLS

Chapter 15

STRANGE MANIFESTATIONS

Before the Kelowna conference, we had seen very few physical manifestations of the Holy Spirit in our lives. When we accept Jesus, no one hands us a manual on what to expect when tongues of fire come and rest upon our heads.

When renewal started in our lives, we wanted to do things in an orderly fashion, but the meetings were anything but orderly. It took us a while to learn what the manifestations meant and to understand what was happening to the people on the floor. Reading about past powerful moves of God, where many of the same manifestations of the Holy Spirit were experienced, helped.

Not everyone experiences the same things while on the floor. Some fall because God powerfully touches them and they experience His love. Others fall because they don't want to be the last person standing – they fall in the flesh, often called a "courtesy fall." For those struggling with demonic oppression, God's anointing can trigger them to manifest demonically while on the floor. While some experience His love, others are healed. While some are sovereignly delivered, others just lay there, not wanting to be left out. This makes our attempts at "orderliness" difficult.

Some manifestations are not difficult to discern. If the manifestation appears sexual or indecent, we know there is a problem. We learned it isn't good if someone screams. To better understand what happens when someone falls under the power of God, we ask questions, often interviewing the person after they come off the floor. What happened to them? What did they experience?

We all like holy laughter, but we only laughed on a couple of occasions. We didn't laugh because someone said, "John 3:16," or some other Scripture. We laughed because of something someone said, or a sound we heard, or something else unusual. We laughed until we thought our sides would burst. It wasn't just laughter; we found we sweat profusely when holy laughter comes. Countless times, we have been asked by people to pray for them so they could laugh, but it is not up to us what you receive. We just stick out our hands and say, "Come, Holy Spirit," and the rest is up to God.

Once, I (Rex) received prayer, fell to the floor, and began to roll from one end of the building to the other. It was strange, and a long way – more than a hundred feet from one side to the other. I just rolled back and forth. I suppose I could have stopped but I was more amazed than alarmed. This must be where they got the term, "Holy roller," I thought to myself. My holy rolling only happened that once, but we have seen it happen to others. In Brazil, we prayed for a church secretary who went down and rolled for what seemed like hours. Two of the church's ushers watched and redirected her so she wouldn't roll off the platform, which was five feet above the main floor.

Once in Toronto, while John Arnott spoke, a man lying on

the floor did the backstroke. He looked like he was swimming around the building. Even John stopped speaking for a couple of minutes and watched this young man as he swam the entire length of the right side, around the back of the platform, and along the left side of the church. He went at least 200 feet without stopping. We watched in amazement as this young man did something that was impossible to do in the natural; he looked like he was in water and effortlessly doing the backstroke.

Manifestations are how the body reacts to what is happening inside an individual when the Holy Spirit comes upon them. When the Argentine pastors came to the United States, they told us we needed to have greater discernment over the manifestations than we had. This led us to watch closely the manifestations that would come upon people.

Normally, when someone cries under the power of God, you might assume they are sad, but that is not always the case. Others laugh and when interviewed tell you they are incredibly sad. Not every manifestation can be easily discerned, so it is imperative that you interview them, both immediately after the manifestation ends and, if possible, again a few days later.

One of the strangest was the "roaring like a lion" manifestation, which began the first year of the revival when John Wimber hosted a meeting at his Anaheim, California, church. A pastor from Asia prophesied that the Lion of Judah was going to devour the dragon over the Asian culture. This resonated with the large Asian contingent who was there. The pastor roared as a prophetic act. This caused many others in the room to roar too, as they agreed with the prophecy. The revival's critics got ahold of it and ran sound bites of people roaring on their radio programs, but didn't offer any context or explanation. Around the world, other people picked up the idea and would randomly roar in a meeting. While it originally had meaning and purpose, the roar became distracting and odd as it spread to other meetings.

KIEV, UKRAINE

After a trip to Russia, we ministered in Kiev, Ukraine. The interpreter assigned to me (Rex) was good and after three days of working together, we had come to understand each other quite well. As one of the evenings turned into early morning, it seemed the crowds pressing in were increasing not decreasing. We had already been praying for close to two and a half hours and there was no end in sight.

A heavy-set grandmother, with a multi-colored scarf covering the thinning hair on her head, came to me for prayer. As my interpreter spoke with her, everyone faded from view. Even the sounds in the room became distant as I could see a new picture superimposed over her. With a little effort, I could switch my view back and forth between the two scenes.

It was the new scene I focused on. I saw the woman sitting, wearing the same dress but no scarf, with an embroidered apron tied around her waist and neck. She sat at a wooden table, a cup of tea in one outstretched hand and the other pressed against her forehead, holding her head up. Her eyes were closed but nothing could keep the sorrow that was so deeply entrenched within her from showing. I could tell her teatime was precious to her, but in my vision not even this special time could hold back the sorrow. I suddenly knew what she was thinking and as quickly as the revelation came to me, the picture left. The noise in the room returned, as if I had come up from underwater. I interrupted my interpreter's conversation with the woman and told her, through the interpreter, what the Holy Spirit had showed me.

For the next few minutes, I told her what I had seen, how she was dressed and what her table and house looked like. I saw a woman standing behind her – she had been at the table too. "You were there," I said. The woman nodded yes. I told her the secret of the sorrow in her heart and let her know that the Lord had revealed it to me so I could tell her that everything was going to be all right. Her friend jumped up and down with excitement. The woman's skin, so wrinkled with tears, brightened up enough for her to smile before she quietly slipped to the floor as the Spirit of God came upon her. A peace came upon that grandmother that had not been there before. Gone were the wrinkles of sorrow and hopelessness; in their place was the peace that surpasses all understanding.

My interpreter said many of the people now wanted me to pray over them, but he refused to tell me what they said. He wanted to see if God would reveal it to me. I prayed and prophesied things that I could have never known without God revealing them to me. Some were healed physically and spiritually, and most fell to the floor.

Such anointed places are rare, and so enjoyable you never want to leave. But it is impossible to operate in that degree of prophetic anointing all the time. However, our understanding of how to cooperate with the Holy Spirit can continue to grow and mature.

OTHER PLACES, OTHER FACES

Sometimes we have noticed more anointing in one physical spot than in another. We encourage prayer team members to find those places and minister in those physical areas. In Englewood, Florida, we walked the platform one Sunday to look and sense in our spirit if such a place could be found. We found one, and asked the worship leader to come and stand in the spot for a few minutes. As he did, he recognized the presence of the Lord. He could hardly play because the presence was so strong on him.

When God truly touches someone, change occurs. We have witnessed people powerfully healed physically and emotionally, and delivered from spiritual bondage. We know people who gave their heart to Jesus while on the floor. When interviewed later, they told us they went through the four spiritual steps you would normally take a person through to receive their salvation – led not by any person, but by the Holy Spirit Himself.

In Brazil, we prayed for a young man who fell to the floor. After a while, he got to his feet, still overwhelmed by the Holy Spirit. We asked if he had been attending all the meetings we held that week and he said he knew nothing about them. He couldn't explain why he was there that night. He was a Catholic and the last thing he remembered was walking down the street to meet some of his friends. As he walked along, he heard the music and, the next thing he knew, he was getting up off the floor after having a very powerful experience with God.

At a series of powerful meetings in Traverse City, Michigan, we noticed attendance grew every night. On the final night, people laid on the floor, completely covering the front of the church. One elderly man, lying in the front, began a very strange and annoying manifestation. As he laid there, he shouted, "HERE

IT COMES! HERE COMES A BIG ONE!" As he yelled, he slowly raised his arms up from his sides until they were above his head. It was like a big ocean wave was washing over him. He did this over and over again; we found it irritating and distracting.

Our irritation must have been evident because a young man came up to us to explain. "That man over there is my father-in-law," he said. "He and his wife are visiting us and this is the first meeting like this they have ever been at, he doesn't do things like this. He's a Baptist." We realized the man was experiencing something quite outside his ability to understand. He was simply enjoying his ride on the wave of the Holy Spirit, as it washed over him again and again.

That Baptist man and his wife became dear friends. For years, they came and helped us with our meetings in the slums of Philadelphia, even though they lived in North Dakota. The Holy Spirit did a mighty work in their lives on the floor in Traverse City and it changed them forever.

I (Lois) have many favorite memories of our experiences throughout the past 20 years of ministry. One stands out to me as it led to a profound change in my life, altering my view of evangelism. I'm still stirred when I think about it and honored to have been there to witness the Holy Spirit draw and move His beloved lost children in such an amazing and powerful way.

We were ministering in a large Ukrainian church with Randy Clark and a small team. The days were full in Ukraine as we ministered twice a day and late into the night. On this particular trip, as well as many of the other trips to this part of the world, God poured out His Spirit in a powerful and phenomenal way. The manifestation of His glory on the people was evident and we were blessed to participate in what the Father was doing. I will never forget the altar call Randy gave that night after his message on God's great love and what the conviction of the Holy Spirit feels like. He talked about the plan of redemption that Jesus made for us and how, through His shed blood, we can be forgiven and made whole. He explained that we must repent of our sins and ask Him to take over our lives as He is the only way that we can be saved. He is the way, the truth, and the life, and there is no other way back to the Father but through Him.

You could feel the heavy presence of God and His conviction come into the room. Randy said when the conviction of the Holy Spirit draws us to come, we need to quit waiting and come now. Every time we turn down the call that He sends us, we harden our hearts more and more until we can no longer feel Him – a spiritually dangerous place to be. Randy counted backwards from 10, and told people to come before he got to 1. Suddenly, masses of people came to the front to receive Jesus Christ as their Savior and Lord. Every age and kind of person came, but what especially tore at my heart were the older Ukrainian women, the "Babushka's," who ran to the front in their long dresses, wearing their aprons and headscarves. They ran with tears streaming down their cheeks and remorse for their sin in their countenances.

What happened then was even more amazing. The people in the crowd stood and cheered for each one, and everyone was in tears and in awe of what God was doing that day. That is how we need to view a sinner coming home: with great joy and anticipation as His arms open wide to all who will come! This is the greatest miracle to witness of all. We were once lost and now we are found, we were blind and now we see! How great is the love our Father has lavished on us who are called His children. One day we will see it all with unveiled faces – every tribe and every nation in His glory worshipping Him as we cry "Holy!"

On another occasion, I (Rex) found myself at a men's retreat held at a camp near the Idaho border. The men were from a church in Spokane and after the pastor spoke, the power of God came. Many of the men had never experienced the degree of anointing that was present that night. The next day, we shared testimonies about what happened the previous evening. I sat on a counter as a group of ten men waited in line to give their testimonies. One man stood out from the rest. He had dark shoulder length hair and was solid muscle. Later, I found out he was the leader of a local chapter of the group called Point Man Ministries, a ministry to Vietnam veterans. The pastor told me the day before he was surprised that any of them were at the meetings, as it was almost impossible to get them to come out for anything.

I sat on the counter and the man stood beside me. Suddenly, I received a vision of him in the jungles of Vietnam. The room didn't disappear, but I had an impression from God showing me something. I saw the man fall asleep on guard duty. While he slept, a Viet Cong enemy slipped into camp and killed a couple of American soldiers. I saw him awaken and, seeing the Viet Cong grab another man, leap upon him. After a fierce struggle, he killed the enemy soldier. The other men in the troop thought he was a hero, but because he knew he had fallen asleep on guard duty, he said nothing. He was bound by grief over falling asleep and he carried the guilt of the men killed, and the lie he lived, every day.

God told me to tell him my vision. God showed me, in detail, that even if he had been awake, he wouldn't have been able to save those other men. I was to tell him that God loved him and did not hold him accountable for the men's deaths. I hopped off the counter, took him aside, and told him what I had seen.

As I told him about my vision, his eyes got big. He didn't stop me nor correct me. Tears ran down his cheeks. I went back and sat on the counter, watching him wipe away the tears as the line for testimonies moved forward. Soon it was his turn to speak. Scattered around the room were the men he had brought from Point Man Ministries; as he spoke, they all leaned forward and listened intently to this man they respected.

Like the soldier he was, he told the story straight out. Since most of the veterans never talk about what happened in Vietnam and rarely revisit old memories, what he said awakened those that came with him. He talked about being on guard duty, falling asleep, the men that were killed, his struggle with the Viet Cong soldier, and killing him. He told how they all thought he was a hero and how he got a medal for bravery. He spoke of the guilt he carried. He confessed his shame for what he did and for misleading his friends and family to think of him as a hero when he was not. As he said this, the men who came with him wove through the crowd to the front. Standing with him, they hugged him and accepted him as only men who have lived through such an experience together can do.

Probably nothing is more controversial in the church than physical manifestations that happen when the Holy Spirit comes in power. People will sometimes tell us they have never manifested but, when asked if they have ever cried during a service, they say yes. For some reason, many people don't think tears are a manifestation like laughter could be.

It wasn't long into the outpouring that a woman came from Brazil to Ruth Hephlin's church and gave her testimony. We watched the video of her giving an incredible, heart-wrenching testimony. As she spoke, a gold-colored substance formed around her. This gold dust, as it was called, was so thick you could see it forming on her, falling off her hair and gathering on her clothes. They tested it and found it was not real gold, but a substance that looked like it. It didn't detract from her testimony but soon this strange occurrence began to happen not just with her but in different places around the world.

Not long afterwards, people reported receiving gold teeth. Old fillings were being changed into bright gold fillings, and people needing fillings were getting gold ones. This was controversial; some quite logically asked if God was doing this, why would He use gold when He could make the tooth perfectly natural, white and whole? Good point, but there were so many people we talked to who claimed the gold in their teeth had not been put there by human hands that we could find no reason to doubt them. However, we noticed that when this phenomenon would occur, the meetings would come to a complete stop as people pulled out tiny pen lights to peer into the mouths of people, trying to see the gold. Honestly, we found that with those little pen lights, every filling took on a gold glare.

All one has to do is read their Bibles and study past moves of God to find even stranger things that have taken place. After all, we have never had a donkey speak to us like Balaam. We have never walked on water like Peter, been swallowed by a whale like Jonah, or seen the Red Sea part so a nation could walk across on dry land. Perhaps what is normal is not normal at all. Perhaps the true reality is what happens to creation and His children when the

King of Kings invades our world. We long to know and experience the unfathomable, faithful love He has for His beloved children. We want to learn to love others as we go from glory to glory, being transformed into His likeness. One day, we will leave this world to live eternally with Him – the greatest manifestation of all. May He be forever praised and exalted as all glory and honor and power belong to Him!

Chapter 16

THE ANOINTING

Intimacy versus Gifting

What is it like to walk into a meeting where the Holy Spirit is moving in power? Perhaps the best way to describe it would be to let someone who came to one of our meetings explain what they experienced.

Betty H. came to a meeting we held in a small church in Perry, Florida, in search of a creative miracle. Paralyzed on the left side from three strokes and partially blind in her left eye, God chose this night to come and touch her. Betty was healed and the following week, she gave her testimony. She started by singing the old hymn, "Oh, He touched me!" The following account is from a tape given to us by the pastor of the church where the miracle happened. It has been transcribed word for word.

BETTY'S CREATIVE MIRACLE

"I have been going through a lot of illness. I have always heard that the closer we get to God the more the devil wants us, one more soul for him. I have gone through one illness after the other. I haven't even been able to attend a church service in a long time. Because the pain in my body and my back has been so severe,

I couldn't sit and attend a service. So we had maintained our living room as our church on Sunday. About two weeks ago, a voice spoke to me and I knew it was the Lord's because I have had Him speak to me before. He told me I was going to church, and I kept asking Him, "How am I going to be able to go to church? How can I go to church in this agony and sit and listen?" But each day He said, "You are going to go to church."

At this time, I began to have real strong chest pain and pressure and the doc had put me on nitroglycerin. Something new was happening and now my heart was getting worse. I told the Lord I didn't know how I was going to make it and he told me I was not going this Sunday but I was to go next Sunday. This kept on for days, over and over again He would say this, the same voice telling me I was going.

I told Jesse what was happening because I couldn't drive, I was partially blind in one eye. I told him the Lord told me we are going to church in two weeks. He said we are not going on Sunday morning, but we are to go Sunday night. I was also told which church we were to go to. I remember it was called Covenant; I had not been in that church for 20 years. But I knew it was the church we were to go to.

Jesse called Pastor Marcus, he said he was not sure they were going to have Sunday night services but later he called me back and told me they had decided to have Sunday night service. I wouldn't have gone if I knew there was something special going on, I couldn't have gotten in front of anyone. The church seemed normal. Everyone greeted us, because of the strokes I have had I know folks but I can't remember their names. The services started and they had a special preacher and halfway through the services I got up and went to the back and leaned against the wall. I hurt so bad I had gone numb on my right side and I was trying to get circulation back. I finally went back and Jesse put my legs up and rubbed them and asked me if we should go home. I said to Jesse, for some reason we need to stay and hear this. I wiggled and squirmed and I hurt and it hurt real bad, it hurt worse than it did for a long time. When it was over I saw people going to the front of the church and I wondered what in the world is going on here what are they doing?

All of a sudden I found myself up front of the church and all these people all over the floor, people everywhere. And I wondered what am I doing up here, what is going on and I found myself standing there and Rex and Lois came over and started praying for me. I don't think I told them anything. I am not aware of what happened from the time I left the pew and got to the front. But, they started praying and the feeling I had was like I was a feather and something had lifted me up and laid me upon the floor. I had fallen in my own house two weeks ago on my back and it hurt so badly, it took a long time to get me up off the floor. But when I landed on that church floor I do not remember making contact. Normally I would have been so embarrassed but I was out for a long time and it felt so good and I still feel so good.

A while later, Jesse said it was well over an hour, I am trying to get off of the floor, people were lying around me laughing, and doing all of these strange things. I am really embarrassed lying on the floor in this church amongst these people. They were trying to get me up but I would find myself back on the floor, my legs were like limp noodles. Finally they got me up into the chair and I realized I could move my right leg. All of a sudden I stood up and two months ago I had been to the doctor because I had been falling a lot. But he said the nerves in my right leg are getting damaged more and more and you are losing circulation and it was ice cold and it stayed ice cold for over 5 years. From the knee to the ankle. And I hadn't said a word yet and when I got up and I found I could bend my knee and my ankle, I had been dragging that leg. The doctor had tried everything to get that leg to move.

I headed to the back but on the way Rex and Lois came up and Rex kneeled down in front of me saying that the Lord had said something to him about my leg, and he took his hands and rubbed my leg vigorously from the knee to the ankle. I had never told him where the most severe pain and numbness was but the heat that came out of his hands – I thought my leg was on fire and it burned so bad but it feels so warm now, just like the other leg. It hasn't felt this good in years since my strokes.

I got to the back and I reached over to the side and touched my husband and it shocked both of us because I couldn't see anything out of the side of my left eye. You had to stand right in front of me for me to see you. But I saw my husband standing at my side and it shocked us both. Then Lois told me to take off my glasses, I thought she was nuts, there was no way I could read this stuff. But I took my glasses off and I started reading and someone said where is she reading, and it wasn't the biggest words but the middle size words I was reading.

I could not understand it, no glasses, my eyes had been healed, my leg had been healed there was no pain in my body anywhere. I have not had any pain in my back worth mentioning, or leg, at all since that night. I have constantly been in sheer agony for six years since my first stroke and been on such severe drugs. I cannot tell you, or think of everything that I have been just healed of. I have had a sore on my foot that has just been oozing from poor circulation for two-and-a-half weeks and it has been healed, it has been healed, it is gone! I cooked for my husband yesterday for the first time in years. My toenails were purple from the bad circulation. They were so bad I hid them cause I was embarrassed but now they have color and they are normal. My chest pain has left me, I couldn't get up and move without severe pain and now it is gone. The only bad thing for my husband has been that now I can go shopping on my own!"

BILL HEARS THE VOICE OF GOD

The next account comes from Bill C., who, with his wife Barbara, came to a meeting we held in Englewood, Florida. This story gives a glimpse into what it's like to be in a meeting where God comes in power to touch, heal and anoint His children.

"After experiencing some delightfully intense and powerful ministry on Friday night when Rex and Lois visited our own Englewood Bible Church, pastor Tony Fiore canceled the Sunday evening service and most of our congregation was present tonight to sit under Rex and Lois Burgher's ministry again, this time at Suncoast Worship Center, where Tom Jones pastors. Again, Rex was in rare form as a gifted storyteller, taking us on a trip down the memory lane of past moves of God. The message that Rex brought tonight was simply to put everything in proper perspective. As humans, we are routinely guilty of a myopic view of God's plans, but when viewed across the panorama of God's landscape, a much different picture emerges. Tonight, Rex deftly wielded that painter's brush, repeatedly dabbing at his palette of many colors to give us a God's-eye view of the historical outpourings the world

has experienced. The message was contained in three parts: Biblical, historical and present day moves of God. Weaving story after story from the Bible and how they must have looked, especially to those who may have been observing them from a distance. Rex has a unique way of bring these stories into contemporary reality. They actually came off the pages in his telling of them.

His knowledge of the facts of church history and the ability to string them together from one story to the next had all of us on the edge of our seats. Many times we were howling with laughter. "We cannot dismiss these miraculous demonstrations of God's power," Rex said. "Neither can we explain them." Even as we tend to dismiss them or even forget the miraculous character of past revivals, history records them as rowdy, demonstrative, and often bizarre in scope. He described events during the Welsh Revival when people reported an 18 inch globe of white light that would come into their church each night and was so bright and warm that they didn't even have to light any gaslights, candles or heat stoves. There were people who were struck with the power of God and who came up off the floor quoting entire chapters of the Old Testament, men who had never laid their eyes on the Bible before. And the story of an 18th century Anglican missionary who described Methodists as a "gang of frantic lunatics, laughing, skipping, dancing, and rejoicing." He described an account from Tommy Reed who watched Jack Coe pray for thirty people who had huge goiters on their necks, and Tommy watched Jack Coe walk down the row of them, slapping the goiters off their necks with his hand, where they fell to the ground and evaporated into thin air, leaving every single person healed. He then went into stories of what he has seen while traveling around the world with Randy Clark, Bill Johnson, Rolland and Heidi Baker, and a host of others. Stories shared often late at night around dinner tables where it is safe to share the incredible phenomena when we go behind the veil.

SOME HEARD THE VOICE OF GOD – OTHERS ASKED "WAS THAT THUNDER?"

"What is all this about?" Rex asked. "It's all to condition us to these very strange and very powerful activities of God so that he can move us up to the next level!" He reminded us of the prophetic word given to Randy Clark and John Arnott, when the Toronto Blessing was becoming known for zaniness and craziness, and Rex had watched it all one night from the balcony – the swooning, the laughing, the falling – all of it causing no small amount of controversy all over the globe. The prophetic word came to Randy and John, "I'm coming to you gently now, so you won't be afraid when I come in power!" Wow! Wow! And yet through it all, some heard the voice of God and saw the reality of His Spirit and understood that it was God – but others are still saying, "Was that thunder I heard?" Throughout the evening, Rex was showing his true colors as a revivalist – the one who constantly reminds us of how God has moved on the earth in years gone by, lest we forget it all completely and God would have to start all over and we would have to employ archaeologists to dig it all up in order to figure out what was really going on. "The power hasn't waned," Rex explained. "God is just getting us used to it so He can take us higher! He's conditioning us!"

Then he called on the Holy Spirit to come and blast us with fire and even while standing in front of my pew, I felt the immediate and powerful touch of Holy Ghost fire tingling my skin. I turned to my wife Barbara and told her "Let's go, let's get up to the front," even as Rex was calling out, "If you are being powerfully touched right now, come on up to the front." Being familiar with the routine, I was already on my way. Barbara stopped as there were people blocking our way out of the row. "Well, you can say EXCUSE ME," I said, knowing that I wanted to get up front while the fire was hot! I was about to leap up onto the seats and jump over the pew when the people moved and we rushed to the front. Rex and Lois were already laying hands on people and they were exploding with the power of God as they flew backwards and sideways and began to pile up quickly. I pushed Barbara to the front where we found Lois already praying for people. As she touched Barbara I heard/felt/perceived? (whether in the body or out I cannot say) a crackling like explosive uncontrollable electricity and we were both knocked off our feet and onto our backs. We lay trembling for some time as the fiery outpouring washed over us. I was undone. I kept my eyes closed as I heard Rex moving around me, praying for others. But even though I couldn't see him with my natural eyes, I could see him in the spirit. It was the strangest scene. In this vision, he had two huge tanks of napalm strapped to his back, just like the flame-thrower at Camp Lejeune during my Marine Corps infantry training. In the natural version, there is a hose coming from the tank with a nozzle that you aim to dispense the napalm. But in the vision, Rex's arm was the hose and his hand was the nozzle. And as he touched each person, fire and flames shot out from the ends of his fingers and seared the people he was praying for with Holy Fire! It was awesome! There's so much more to see, so much more understanding when you're seeing from a supernatural perspective than from a natural one.

This went on for some time, with Holy Ghost-blasted bodies everywhere, finally transitioning to a fire tunnel (well of course) and a time of worship, praise, dancing and just frolicking in the Holy Ghost. It was just wonderful. We praised and danced until we were all exhausted and finally things began to wind down.

Rex had done such a great job of bringing everything together for us -- to see all of this from God's perspective and not from our own. To expand our vision from an earthly one into a heavenly one. So now we all with eager anticipation, look forward to the next wave of God's glory and wonder what will it be like? But then, we have all heard the voice from Heaven. Unfortunately there are some who are still asking, "Hey, was that thunder I heard?"

WALKING IN INTIMACY AND UNDER THE ANOINTING

Since 1995, we have had the privilege of living in an incredible time of a visitation from God. It was a blessing to be touched by God so powerfully that we continually shook under that anointing for months and months. Unbelievable visions and dreams, along with amazing opportunities to pray for people, came to us one right after the other, filling our lives with a bounty of experiences. We were, and still are, living with a book of Acts experience.

Later, when many experienced a decrease in manifestation, the Lord gave us the privilege of traveling and working alongside Randy Clark. For three intense years, it was a daily experience to pray for hundreds, if not thousands, of people. It was a privilege to live in an anointing that very few people get to experience on a daily basis. Now that we are out on our own ministering, we have been blessed to continually feel the river of His presence in our lives.

There is a big difference in being in a continual state of anointing while ministering and having a personal relationship with Jesus. They are two different things altogether. When you operate in the gifts that God has blessed you with, there can be a very powerful anointing that comes. That anointing is not a substitute for having a continual relationship with the Father. There is a similarity between the two – both are experiences that can be felt physically, but that is as close as they come.

When we were touched so powerfully in 1995, two things happened to us. One was that we received a personal revelation of the Father's love for us. We fell in love with Him all over again. It may have been that we saw Him for the first time because we cannot remember ever loving Him so much. It was truly a restoration of our first love.

The second thing was an incredible anointing came on the gifting that God had blessed us with during the preceding 14 years of our walk with Him. It seemed like we had been elevated from a Grade 3 to college level anointing when it came time to pray for the sick. We also experienced a depth of revelation in dreams and visions as if we passed from looking through a glass darkly to seeing with incredible clarity. From that day onward, we enjoyed an incredible feeling of swimming in liquid love every time we ministered in His name.

The anointing of God on the intimacy of our relationship with Him and the anointing on the gifts is a powerful combination that too few of us ever walk in successfully.

Sadly, the anointing of gifting is easier to maintain than the anointing that comes out of our relationship with Him. One would think it would be the same, but it's not. From time to time, we heard people say to those touched by God, "When are you going to get up off the floor and do something?" When were we going to go and save the lost, heal the sick, raise the dead and do the "stuff," as John Wimber used to say? But in Luke 10:17-20, when Jesus met with His excited followers who came back full of stories about what they had done, He told them, "Do not rejoice that the spirits submit to you, but rejoice that your names are in heaven!" In other words, having demons submit to you and seeing people saved, healed and delivered out of your gifting is good – but even more exciting is that you and your Father in Heaven are in relationship.

The greatest revelation and experience we can have in life is to know, and be known by, our Father God. As Paul wrote in 1 Corinthians 13, *"And these things remain; faith, hope, and love, but the greatest of these is love."* It still comes down to the basics: will you make the time to climb into the lap of the One who loves you, look into His eyes and find your place of perfect rest? It doesn't matter if you are used powerfully. What matters is learning to abide continually in His love. Through all of the amazing experiences and places we have been, we have discovered the best thing is to know Him, remain in His love, and live out of the fullness of that love. Neglecting such a great love breaks the heart of God.

We have heard many people, used mightily by the Holy Spirit, say they are dry and in need of another infilling from God. That should come as no surprise. From the greatest to the smallest, the challenge has always been the same: God chooses intimacy over ministry every time. That's why Paul said in 1 Corinthians 13 that those who choose gifting over relationship are in danger of becoming a *"resounding gong or a clanging cymbal."*

There is a yearning in our hearts for "Abba Daddy" to hold us. We were created for relationship and intimacy with our Lord. May we be ones that remember, even in the midst of great power and anointing, to keep our priorities in His order. Our desire and our prayer should be one:

Father God, if You should visit us so powerfully again, we will choose relationship and intimacy over all else. Set out our priorities according to your order: intimacy and relationship with You first and foremost; pure and honorable love for our spouses, flowing out of intimacy with You; and showing Your protective and nurturing love for our children and families. Then, Lord, may we not forget to minister to those You send us to. Keep us from putting ministry before all else. Help us to keep it in perspective – let us choose the anointing of being with our God over the anointing of doing the "stuff."

The first and greatest commandment is this: *"Love the Lord your God with all your heart and with all your soul and with all your mind, and the second is like it – love your neighbor as yourself."*

Daddy, we love You so much. Amen.

EPILOGUE

Randy Clark proclaimed from the outset that this was a revival of 'little old me's!' and for many of us, the thought that we could be used supernaturally by God was beyond anything we ever imagined. In 1995, through the laying on of hands, the Holy Spirit came upon us both in power, leading us to 19 countries to spread the fire of His love through signs and wonders. The anointing we received was an anointing of the power to save, heal and deliver individuals. What we experienced became the norm for our lives and from church to church we have been blessed to see the same anointing that touched us and changed our lives come and touch thousands of others – some who, like us, now travel the world spreading the good news of Jesus Christ.

This book cannot possibly contain everything that we have experienced these past 20 years. We left out so much of what we were blessed to be a part of. To be present when Randy interviewed four men under the Bakers' ministry in Mozambique as they told us what it was like to raise people from the dead was an honor. To be anonymously whisked around China to meet and interview the top leaders of China's underground church and then to receive prayer from these humble men and women was overwhelming. We will never forget being asked to speak at the largest Messianic church in Europe, where we experienced the most powerful sense of His presence. What a blessing it has been to sit long into the night listening to the saints who are being used powerfully around the world speak of the supernatural things they have witnessed. What a privilege to listen to men and women who sat under people like Smith Wigglesworth, Jack Coe and others, share their experiences. From walking the garbage dumps with Heidi and Rolland to meeting and ministering with the humble pastors who treated us with such honor and hospitality as they set exquisite homemade meals before us in small towns scattered throughout the Ukraine, we have been truly blessed beyond what we could ever imagine.

Some are asking when the next wave of His presence is coming to the Church. Though no one is sure of the exact time, we do know that our Heavenly Father has not grown tired of loving His children and the anointing of the 'Father's blessing' is still available to all those who are dry and thirsty and desire a fresh touch from Him.

Our lives were forever changed when we said yes to our Father. Our daughters, the Godly men they married, and each of our six grandchildren carry our heritage of saying 'yes' to God. We pray that this book will encourage you to say 'yes' to our Father, seek His face and see what God will do to and through you, as you press in and run the race He has designed especially for you.

God bless you, and may you be in His love always.

About the Authors

Rex & Lois Burgher are authors and international conference speakers with a passion to see people's lives transformed into the image of God.

Rex & Lois have been happily married for 38 years. They have two daughters and six grandchildren.

In 2001, Rex and Lois co-founded Kingdom Life Ministry in Dillsburg, Pennsylvania. Together they have ministered in over nineteen nations around the world. Their story reverberates in the hearts of all those who desire to be used by God. Their lives speak of ones who have dared to step out of their comfort zone and say "yes" to God.

Rex is the author of two books: *Journey to your Kingdom Destiny* and *Our Father's Heartbeat*.

Kingdom Life Ministries Presentations:

For seminars, retreats or other speaking engagements, contact Rex & Lois at the KLM Offices

PO Box 583
Dillsburg, PA 17019
(717) 502-0343 or email
info@klifemin.org

MORE FROM REX & LOIS BURGHER

Come along on an adventure into the heart of our Father. From the breathtaking days of creation to the epic return of Jesus, you will be introduced to the original Heartbeat of home.

"Rex skillfully lays out the plan of the ages, embracing the assignment that Jesus left us—reconcile people to the Father."
                                        Bill Johnson

(Foreword by Dr. Randy Clark)

"A faith-building, reliable guidebook that will take you straight to your highest destiny."
                               Rolland & Heidi Baker
"You will be challenged and encouraged with much grace and strength to come into your God-ordained destiny."
                                        Bill Johnson
"An important roadmap to your understanding, believing in, and accomplishing your kingdom destiny."
                                     Dr. Randy Clark

'Our Father's Heartbeat'
'Journey to your Kingdom Destiny'
'When The Fire Falls'

Publications of:

KINGDOM LIFE MINISTRY

To Order Additional Books:
On Line, By Phone or by Mail:

On-line
www.klifemin.org

Phone:
717-502-0343

Mail:
Kingdom Life Ministries
PO Box 583
Dillsburg, PA 17019, USA
(include a check for $15.99 + $3.00 for shipping and handling)

40% Discounts will be given to purchases of **5** or more books:
Phone: 717-502-0343
Email: info@klifemin.org